Nimble Numeracy

Fluency in Counting and Basic Arithmetic

Phyllis E. Fischer, Ph.D.

Oxton House Publishers
Farmington, Maine

18.95

Oxton House Publishers, LLC
P. O. Box 209
Farmington, Maine 04938
phone: 1-800-539-7323
fax: 1-207-779-0623
www.oxtonhouse.com

Publisher's Cataloging-in-Publication
(Provided by Quality Books, Inc.)

Fischer, Phyllis E.
    Nimble numeracy : fluency in counting and basic
arithmetic / Phyllis E. Fischer. – 1st ed.
    p. cm.
    Includes index.
    ISBN: 1-881929-19-1

    1. Arithmetic–Study and teaching (Elementary)
2. Numeracy–Study and teaching (Elementary) 3. Teaching–
Aids and devices. I. Title.

QA135.5.F58 2002   372.7′2′044
                              QBI02-200280

Printed in the United States of America

09 08 07 06 05 04 03 02   10 9 8 7 6 5 4 3 2 1

Preface

I have taught courses and given workshops on automaticity and fluency in reading since the mid-1970s. While talking with students, parents, teachers, and other professionals about developing automatic skills, the problem of automaticity and fluency in arithmetic has often come up. Many (if not most) students who have difficulty becoming fluent at the reading task also have great difficulty memorizing the basic arithmetic facts. Many of them also have trouble becoming fluent with our counting system. This often results in such learning problems as slow learning of arithmetic concepts, slow processing of arithmetic problems, and inaccurate computations even when the algorithms are known.

As we talked about these problems I would describe how I make speed drills for practice on basic arithmetic facts, and I would talk about how extremely important it is to have fluency with the language of our counting system. Teachers often reminded me that their lives are so busy that they don't have time to create these materials themselves, which aren't part of regular arithmetic programs and aren't available for general use. Parents were also clamoring for materials to use. In response to these requests for materials, I have written this book, and also a set of speed drills for arithmetic facts.

This book explains how to teach our counting system, how to work with the base-ten place-value system, how to teach adding and subtracting as related operations, and how to teach multiplying and dividing as related operations. A major emphasis is on developing fluent use of the language needed for working in these areas and for communicating with other people about these skills and concepts.

The activities presented in this book are easy to do with individuals, small groups, or whole classrooms of students. Suggested wording for the teacher is included, but it is not intended to be a script that must be followed. Some teachers use almost the exact wording suggested; others paraphrase extensively. Teachers have said that they like to have suggested wording because it is the clearest explanation of what is to be done and what is expected of the students. Only very basic materials are needed for the activities and, other than ordinary things to count, displays of the required materials are included in the book for photocopying by any teacher, parent, or tutor.

Acknowledgments

It seems as though I am always apologizing for not remembering names; these acknowledgments would be very incomplete without mention of some wonderful people whose names I don't remember. First, I thank my third grade teacher. Under her careful guidance, armed with toothpicks and string, we manipulated problems and number patterns so clearly and quickly that mathematics became a most inviting world. The activities we did were just as effective with my own third graders as they had been with me, and some of them are carried on into this book. My high school mathematics teachers were brave enough to challenge us with mathematical ideas and patterns that were not normally included in high school textbooks.

My third graders in Hopkins, Minnesota, showed me how important it is to become fluent on the number system and to memorize number facts, things that were not at all in vogue when I began teaching in the 1960s. I also thank the people in the Hopkins school district who introduced me to the work of Maria Montessori, Georges Cuisenaire, Caleb Gattegno, and Zoltan Dienes and asked me to teach a remedial arithmetic class in the summer. Those sessions were videotaped and, though the purpose for the videotapes was to help other teachers learn how to use Cuisenaire Rods, the process helped me refine my teaching and showed me how valuable videotaping is for one's own professional development. (It was, no doubt, good that they didn't tell me about the videotaping until I had agreed to teach the class!)

The professionals and parents with whom I've worked have given me feedback, ideas, and advice that are invaluable. Finally, I want to thank my husband, who is a mathematician. In addition to providing constant encouragement, he makes sure my teaching ideas and the words I use are mathematically sound.

Contents

First Thoughts

As I watched my third graders become proficient at adding and subtracting, it always seemed to me that proficiency came when they saw how the three numbers in an addition/subtraction statement were connected to each other — for instance, when they saw that 2, 3, and 5 are related by $2 + 3 = 5$ and $5 - 2 = 3$ and $5 - 3 = 2$. The same thing was true for multiplying and dividing. Proficiency came once they saw the relationships between statements such as $5 \times 2 = 10$ and $10 \div 5 = 2$. Watching children for whom even the simple number facts were difficult, it seemed that just working on such triples of numbers wasn't enough to develop the automaticity that would make arithmetic easy. Those children also seemed to lack automaticity on basic counting sequences, or "counting chants," as I prefer to call them.

These observations indicate that there are two different kinds of activities which are particularly helpful for students who have difficulty memorizing the basic number facts. One such activity is counting, which develops fluency with the very basic notions of sequences and patterns of numbers and with the words that represent them. The other is working on the triples of numbers in addition and subtraction, and later in multiplication and division. These activities are the focus of the materials presented in this book.

Activities for students who have difficulty memorizing basic number facts are useful for all students. Automaticity at basic tasks is the hallmark of proficient performance, whether the performance is doing mathematics, or reading, or writing, or playing a sport. Automaticity should be a goal of every teacher for every student.

Because these materials are intended to be useful for teachers of students who are having difficulty as well as for students who are flying through their lessons, they are organized by topic, not by day. If you are a teacher, this means that you will have to become familiar with the materials and will have to evaluate a student's skills to determine which materials will be useful when teaching the student. Additionally, you will need to make some basic teaching decisions in relation to the following considerations:

- The amount of material that can be covered in one lesson will depend on how easily the students are learning it and how long they can attend to the task.

- When to switch from one set of activities to another will depend on your judgment of what is most useful for the students. Young students have different needs and skills than do older students, and all students come with different knowledge, skills, and abilities. Suggestions are given in the materials, but you, the teacher, are the best judge of this.

- The concepts and skills covered in the regular mathematics program must be taught. The amount of time that should be spent on these automaticity activities will depend on how you decide to integrate the two. Additionally, if the teaching methodologies conflict, you will have to decide which ones to use, based on the rationales provided and your own experience with your students.

In all of these materials, a major focus is on developing fluency with language. Many students who are not fluent in mathematics cannot use the language of mathematics at an automatic level. Some of them have basic language processing and/or production problems and require lots and lots of carefully designed practice in order to develop the required fluency. Others just have not learned and practiced the language of mathematics or the relationship of mathematical language to everyday language. Many students have memorized (or tried to memorize) rules by which they can solve arithmetic equations. They have not been taught how the equations represent problems, nor have they learned to start with the problems and develop the mathematical statements that represent the problems.

Most students come to school with a great deal of mathematical knowledge. They need to learn how users of mathematics talk about and represent that knowledge. The everyday language of the world from which the students come must be connected to the mathematical language and symbolism common to the sciences and the many other areas that use mathematical tools. A mathematics teacher I know once told a group of administrators that he is bilingual, and one of his languages is a universal language — mathematics. The job of every teacher of mathematics is to be sure their students are truly bilingual, which means that they can go back and forth between the language of mathematics and the language of their everyday world.

The following pages focus on two types of activities. As you read them to evaluate which sections you will use with different students, think about each student's automaticity with the language patterns. It may be that some who are having trouble with math really know the concepts, but need the practice on the language that these materials provide.

Type 1: Counting Automaticity

- Under this heading, Chapters 2 – 9 are for teaching the numbers, beginning with the teen numbers. I focus on the patterns of the numbers and develop the concepts relating to the number system. Additionally, I provide activities for fast oral and written practice that will develop the basic counting chant automaticity that so many students have not yet mastered. I recommend that you consider going quickly through these activities even if your students can count to 100. Many teachers have said that going quickly through these materials has really helped their students understand the pattern of our number system.

- Chapters 10 and 11 suggest a variety of counting activities. These activities help students become fluent on patterns in the numbers, which helps them with many mathematical tasks, such as adding and subtracting, multiplying and dividing, and estimating.

Type 2: Number Fact Automaticity

- Chapters 12 – 14 are for teaching students the connection between the various basic arithmetic operations. They begin with the relationship between addition and subtraction, so that students can become automatic at all of the addition, subtraction, and missing addend statements which can be written for three particular numbers (e.g., 4, 5, and 9). The connection between multiplication and division is also taught and is expanded to fractions.

- Related to this set are my *Speed Drills for Arithmetic Facts* (Oxton House, 2001). Addition, subtraction, and missing addends are in one section. Multiplication, division, and basic fractions are in another section. If your students already understand the relationships taught in Chapters 12 and 13, you can have them begin these speed drills without going through those materials. The speed drills will not teach the concepts presented in this book, however, so don't start with the speed drills if your students do not know the concepts.

Counting to 19

Parents and teachers know that learning to chant the numbers from 1 to 10 is one of the skills that young children are typically very eager to master. Indeed, most children enter kindergarten able to count 10 objects. Many children can count well beyond that, but some struggle to remember the names one, two, three, four, and five in the correct order. Of course, the sooner the children learn to count, the faster they will learn arithmetic. There are many, many good descriptions of activities that will help young children learn to count and this booklet is not intended to cover that material. The activities in this book are designed to expand upon your students' presumed ability to count at least to 10 and to recognize those basic numerals.

I use a chart for teaching the counting chant and the connection between our oral English counting words, the numerals we write them with, and our place value system. This chart, which I call a *counting chart*, and a blank chart for student work are included as foldout blackline masters at the end of this book.

Many arithmetic materials contain this type of chart. When I was teaching third grade (some years ago), all of them that I saw had the multiples of ten (10, 20, 30, ...) in the leftmost column; now it seems that the majority of them have the multiples in the rightmost column. I am very fussy about wanting these numbers in the *left* column. A *ten* is *ten* ones, but it is also *one* ten and *zero* ones. *Zero* ones does not come after *nine* ones; *zero* ones comes before *one* one. Because we rename or regroup when we go from nines to tens, I want the row change on the chart to come at that point. When we talk about "the twenties," we don't mean 21 through 30; we mean 20 through 29. I want these numbers to be on one line, starting with 20. All the illustrations in this book match my counting chart.

The chart goes up to 139 because many students need to see numbers well past 100 in order to become fluent at thinking about the pattern of repeating the numbers from *one* to *one hundred* in the extension of the counting chant to larger and larger numbers.

Learning the Numbers 11 through 19

11 and 12   (If your students can name these numbers automatically in any context and can write them accurately whenever they hear or say them, skip to the next section. Read through this section, however, for specific instructions on fast practice in recognizing, naming, and writing the numbers; the activities will be repeated with other numbers.)

Materials needed besides pencils and paper:

- A counting chart on which you have 1 to 9 on one row and 10 to 12 on the second row, as follows:

	1	2	3	4	5	6	7	8	9
10	11	12							

- Similar (but smaller) counting charts for your students on which you have written "10 11 12" in a size appropriate for their handwriting.

- For each student, individual cards on which you have written the numerals 10, 11, and 12, one on each card.

- Things to count. In addition to loose objects, I like to use patterned materials such as dominoes or any of the arithmetic blocks, such as Cuisenaire rods or Unifix cubes. The 10 block in such sets stays constant, so you can focus on 11 and 12 without having to recount up to 10.

If you need to teach *eleven* and *twelve*, show the students your chart and say something like:

> Today we're going to work on the numbers *ten, eleven,* and *twelve.* Look here. (Point to 10.)
>
> I have written the *ten.* The next number after *ten* is *eleven.* Say *eleven.* (*"eleven"*)
>
> The next number is *twelve.* Say *twelve.* (*"twelve"*)
>
> Let's say them as I point to them. Point and say the names two or three times.

Give each of your students cards with 10, 11, and 12 written on them. Ask them to point to the number you name, saying the numbers in random order. (If you are working with a large group, the students can hold up the appropriate card.) After the first two commands of Point to ___, you can just say the number name. Going quickly, you can have them point to each number four or five times in a minute. Then ask them to look up at your chart and name the number you point to (in random order). Again, going quickly, you can ask them to name each number four or five times in a minute. At first, say the name with them if they need you to. This must be absolutely accurate because it is a plain memorization task.

With their cards in front of them, have them trace the number you name with their fingers or the eraser end of a pencil. First, name the numbers in order. Then repeat them in random order a few times.

In the next lesson, repeat the activities quickly and, after your students have traced the numbers a couple of times, have them write them as you dictate. Repeat whichever parts of these steps are necessary for as many days as are necessary for your students to be able to

▷ name the numbers consistently and fluently (within two seconds) when they see them in any situation (e.g., on the clock or in books),

▷ write them accurately when you dictate them, and also

▷ put the individual number cards in order.

If your students know how to read *two*, draw attention to the fact that you have written the 12 below the 2 because they both have 2 in them, and write the word *twelve* below the word *two* to show that these names both begin with *tw*. You may need to discuss the fact that we don't hear the /w/ in *two*; that's part of what makes it an outlaw word (or whatever you call the irregular words). If they do not know how to read *two*, don't draw their attention to this, lest they confuse *ten* and *twelve* because both words start with /t/.

Have the students count objects or actions to match the numbers one-to-one with concrete items. At first, I have them count out ten objects and put the number card with 10 above the group. They then count out eleven objects and put the number card 11 above the group; they repeat with twelve objects. I then have them start with a 10 pattern (a domino, the orange Cuisenaire rod, 10 Unifix cubes connected, etc), putting it below the group of ten items. Then they put a 10 pattern plus a 1 under the 11, counting ten, eleven. Continue with the 12. Some students need lots of practice with this; others can count objects automatically as soon as they know the names of the numbers in the correct order (the counting chant).

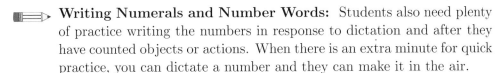 **Writing Numerals and Number Words:** Students also need plenty of practice writing the numbers in response to dictation and after they have counted objects or actions. When there is an extra minute for quick practice, you can dictate a number and they can make it in the air.

Reading and Writing the Number Words: Students should learn to read and write the number words (*one, two, three,* etc.) as soon as they can. However, these arithmetic activities are certainly appropriate for first grade children who can count to ten but can't read or write words. My experience is that young children love arithmetic if they can understand it. They often find it easier than reading and writing. At the same time, it is important for students to learn to read and write these words, and the spelling of the words will help them learn the patterns of the number system. I work on the numbers as quickly as the children can learn them, and I bring in reading and writing the number words as soon as they know the basic letter-sound relationships. (I follow the same guidelines for some older, severely dyslexic children.) Where there are suggestions for reading and writing the number words, use your knowledge of your students to decide when you can have them do these tasks.

An early activity for students who are not yet reading and writing very much is to have the numeral and number word on a card that can be traced as the word is pronounced. As soon as your students know the sounds for the consonants and some of the vowels, begin to draw their attention to the spelling and sound patterns of the number words as they trace them.

13 through 19

Materials needed besides pencils and paper:

- A counting chart with 1 – 9 on the first row and 10 – 19 on the second row.

- Small counting charts for your students on which you have written "13 14 15 16 17 18 19" in a size appropriate for their handwriting. You can add these numbers to the previous chart if you have just finished working on 10, 11, and 12. I often write 13 and 15 in a different color to help remind them that they have names slightly different than the related 3 and 5.

- For each student, individual cards on which you have written the numerals 13 through 19, one on each card.

- Things to count, including patterned materials such as dominoes or any of the arithmetic blocks, such as Cuisenaire rods or Unifix cubes.

With your chart out, introduce the lesson by pointing to each number while saying something like:

Today we're going to work on the numbers *thirteen, fourteen, fifteen, sixteen, seventeen, eighteen,* and *nineteen.* That's a lot all at once, but you really know them already because you know the numbers *three* (point to 3 above 13), *four* (continue to point as you name them), *five, six, seven, eight,* and *nine.*

Let's start with *fourteen.* We say the *four* first, and then say *teen* for the *one* that's right before it. Point to the 4 and 1 as you say this. Point to the 4 and 1 while you say *four* and *teen* again. Pause very slightly between the syllables.

Now you say it while I point to the numbers. (*"four teen"*) Again. (*"four teen"*) Again. (*"fourteen"*).

The student should say the word with no pause by the last time.

Now let's try this one. Point to 19.

Point to the 9 above 19 and say, This is *nine,* so for this (point to 19) we say *nine teen.* Point to the 9 and then the 1 as you say the words.

Say it with me. Have them say the words two or three times as you point. Say it with them if they need it.

Now you do this one. (Point to 18.)

These are the same (point to the two 8s) so you'll say that and then add *teen.* Say the number when I point.

Point and have them say *eight teen* two or three times.

Repeat with 16 and 17. Then have the students name 14, 16, 17, 18, and 19. (If you do not have enough time or focus of attention to go through all of the numbers, this is a good place to stop introducing them. Go to the step below of having the students point to, read, and trace them on their own cards. If you stop here, review these numbers briefly before you introduce 13 and 15, which are next.)

Introduce 13 by pointing to it and saying something like:

> Now we'll work on *thir teen*. It's just a little harder because we say *thir* instead of *three*. Say *thir*. (*"thir"*) Again. (*"thir"*)
>
> So, this number (point to 13) is *thirteen*. What is it? (*"thirteen"*)
>
> We say *thir* for this part of *thir teen*. Point to the 3 in 13. What number does it match? (Point to the 3 above.) (*"three"*)
>
> So we say *thir* for the 3 and *teen* for the 1 (point). Say the number. (*"thirteen"*) Again. (*"thirteen"*)

Repeat with 15, comparing *five* with *fif*.

 Fast Oral Practice: You say *thir* and they say *three*, you say *fif* and they say *five*, you say *three* and they say *thir*, or you say *five* and they say *fif*.

Give the students their cards containing the numbers 13 through 19 and have them point to the numbers you name. Have them name the numbers you point to. Have them trace the numbers while saying them. They can also order the cards from smallest to largest saying the numbers as they order them.

When there is a minute for fast practice (e.g., as they line up to go somewhere or as you change activities) say one of the *teen* numbers and have the students tell you the single number that matches it. When that is fluent, say the single number and have them tell you the *teen* number that matches. Also dictate numbers and have them make them in the air.

Practice counting objects in the same way as for 10, 11, and 12. In addition to counting objects, students need fast oral practice on a couple of other counting tasks:

▷ They should be able to tell you the next number up from any number you say or show them. For example, you say *seven* and they say *eight*, or you say *thirteen* and they say *fourteen*. As you add more numbers to their counting charts, continue to practice this skill.

▷ I also like them to count up <u>two</u> from any number I say or show them. I like to have them say the first number quietly and the second number louder. For instance, I say *eight* and they say *nine*, **ten**; I say *eleven*, they say *twelve*, **thirteen**. This emphasis seems to help them learn these steps quite easily. Of course, counting by twos (the even numbers) will help even more. (See Chapter 10, Skip Counting.) Over many years, I have observed only a couple of students who were unable to count up two steps quickly and easily, emphasizing the second number.

▷ The students should also be able to tell you one number lower than the one you say or show them. For example, you say *seven* and they say *six*, or you say *sixteen* and they say *fifteen*. For many students, this might become automatic only when they can easily visualize the counting chart or some other pattern for the numbers.

Writing Numerals and Number Words: You say the numbers and the students say and write them. Have them write them in the air as they are changing activities, walking in the hall, etc.

Have the students match numbers to their written names. You say the numbers and the students say them, segment the words into sounds, and write the words, tracing them first, if necessary.

Place Value for the *-teen* Numbers

When your students can count up to 19 objects, can name all the numerals and read the words, and can tell you which of the numerals is matched with *teen* and which part is matched with *thir*, *four*, *fif*, etc., (and the reverse), it is time to introduce place value. The names for the numbers make much more sense when they understand *ones* and *tens*. I use counting sticks for an activity "game" that is included in most good books on teaching mathematics.

Materials needed besides pencils and paper:

• For each student, make a file folder. At the top of one side, write "ones," and at the top of the other, write "tens." I call this a *place value folder*.

- For each student, have about 25 counting sticks and a few holders for bundling the counters into tens. (Popsicle or stirring sticks and rubber bands work, but I prefer strips of construction paper and paper sleeves to hold them. If you cut the construction paper into strips about 3 inches long and a half-inch wide, you can use the paper wrappers for $10 worth of dimes as the sleeves. Cut the wrappers into half-inch pieces to get several sleeves out of each wrapper.)

- For yourself, prepare a few charts you can write on. (I call them *place value charts* or *tens|ones charts.*) You'll want to save them for the students to look at as you work, so have a couple of extras handy for review or for working with a student who doesn't understand what you have just done. On the right half of the paper, put a *tens* column and a *ones* column with a line separating them. To the left of that, put lines to write numbers on. (See Display 2-1.)

Give each student the folder labeled *ones and tens*, the counting sticks, and the wrappers. Explain that there are only two rules for the game. One is that whenever we get ten sticks on the *ones* side we have to bundle them and move them to the *tens* side. The other (which is really a result of the previous one) is that we can put only unbundled sticks on the *ones* side and only bundled sticks on the *tens* side. Then have them show you lots of numbers. For example, you might start with:

How many ones?	tens	ones
_____	____	____
_____	____	____
_____	____	____
⋮	⋮	⋮

Display 2-1

> **Show me seven sticks.** Write 7 on a sheet of paper or the board while you say it.

If the students don't quickly put them on the *ones* side of the folder, say something like,

> **Since we can't bundle ten sticks, we have to put the seven sticks on the *ones* side.** (Point.)

If the students readily put the sticks under the *ones*, confirm that they are under the *ones* because they have only seven sticks so they can't bundle any. Then say something like,

> **So we have seven sticks on the *ones* side. We can say that we have *seven ones*.**

Continue with several other single-digit numbers, emphasizing that we can call them ___ ones. Then put sticks on the *ones* side and have the students tell you how many you have, using "ones" in their answer. You can keep writing the numbers on paper, or switch to identifying them on the first row of the counting chart. Do several examples.

Next work on the *teen* numbers. Say something like:

Now show me *fourteen* sticks.

Write the number 14 on the prepared place value chart, to the left of the place value columns. Have them put the sticks on the ones side of the place value folder. Ask,

Now what was our rule about when we have to bundle up the sticks and put the bundle on the *tens* side? (*"When we have ten sticks we have to bundle them up and put the bundle on the tens side."*) Help them with the rule, if necessary.

Good. We have the same number of sticks; we just bundled them differently. We had fourteen *ones* and we bundled them so we have *one* ten and *four* ones. Watch while I write that.

Next to the 14, write a 1 in the *tens* column and a 4 in the *ones* column.

Let's do another one. Clear your folders.

Repeat the process with some of the other *teen* numbers. If no one volunteers that the 1 in the *tens* column is called *teen*, draw their attention to it by pointing to the place value columns and saying something like:

All of these numbers have some *ones* and a *ten*, but when we tell how many things there are altogether, do we use the word *ten*? (*"No."*)

No, we don't. What do we call the *ten*? (*"teen"*)

That's right, we use the word *teen*. We say the *ones* and then say *teen* for the *one ten*.

Tell your students a *teen* number and have them tell you how many ones and tens it can be bundled in. Tell them how many ones and tens you have and have them tell you the *teen* number it will be if the *ten* is unbundled. If they need to look at the ones and tens columns on the chart or folder to do this, that's fine. They won't need it for very long.

Next work on 10, 11, and 12. Write the number 10 to the left of the *tens|ones* columns and say something like:

> Now we're going to tell how many ones and tens there are in the numbers *ten, eleven,* and *twelve.* Let's start with *ten.* Show me ten sticks. Wait while they show you.
>
> Do you have to bundle them? (*"Yes."*)
>
> Good. So how many ones do you have left over? (*"none"* or *"zero"*)
>
> So when I write it up here, I'll put a 0 in the ones column and a 1 in the tens column. Draw their attention to the name by saying,
>
> When we say *ten,* we don't say anything for the *zero* ones, do we. We just call the whole thing *ten.*
>
> Let's see if we can do *eleven* without counting sticks. Look here while I write 11. Write it to the left of the *tens|ones* column.
>
> Point to 11 and say, How many would you bundle? (*"ten"*)
>
> So how many bundles of ten do we have? (*"one"*)
>
> Good; I'll write 1 in the tens column. How many ones are left over? Point to the 11. (*"one"*)
>
> Good; I'll write 1 in the ones column. So we have *one* ten and *one* one. If we unbundle the ten, how many ones do we have altogether? (*"eleven"*)

Repeat with 12.

 Fast Oral Practice: Describe the numbers with the tens bundled and unbundled as described above.

A word of caution: I have watched many children fill in worksheets that have the place value columns with the number expressed as *ones* written on the line to the left, like the one you have just used. Although the intent is that the children will practice thinking that 18, for example, is 1 ten and 8 ones as they write the 1 in the tens column and the 8 in the ones column, they can complete the worksheet just by copying the numbers, even while carrying on an unrelated conversation! If you think your students need independent practice on this, have them do a few (perhaps five) examples that ask for tens and ones in a random order, something like this:

- In 18 we have ___ tens and ___ ones.

- In 16 we have ___ ones and ___ tens.

- In 12 we have ___ ones and ___ tens.

You can also ask for just one of the places:

- In 17, how many tens do we have? ___

- In 14, how many ones do we have? ___

- In 19, how many ones do we have? ___

 Many people use beans glued to a stick for the tens and single beans for the ones. When the students have ten or more beans they trade them in for a stick of ten beans. I have found that young children and students who are having trouble with mathematics learn these concepts better if they actually bundle the sticks into tens. Later, when they begin regrouping in addition and subtraction, they will both make bundles and take bundles apart. They seem to understand the concept of the regrouping more easily than if they have to exchange a certain number of beans for sticks with beans on them or vice versa. It seems as though the exchanging is an extra step that doesn't match what we do when we write the problems. It also seems as though some students think of it as a different number when they have exchanged beans for a stick.

The idea of a number being represented in different ways cannot be overemphasized. Students need to be flexible in the way they think about numbers. Furthermore, they will need to be able to "regroup" for many calculations they need to do both in school and in life experiences.

The concept of regrouping depends on understanding that a number can be represented in different ways without changing value. In base ten, we bundle and unbundle when we get to tens: ten ones, ten tens, ten hundreds, etc. Thus, 72 can be represented as unbundled ones (72 of them), as 7 bundles of ten and 2 ones, as 6 bundles of ten and 12 ones, etc. When we "borrow," as so many of our math materials call it, we are not borrowing from an unrelated number, we are unbundling a number and representing it with a different number of tens and ones, or hundreds and tens, etc. Although this may seem nit-picky, it is the foundation for why we regroup. If all students know is the rote procedure for "borrowing" or "carrying," they cannot do the problem solving they need to do to correct errors or see alternative ways of solving problems. This deprives them of the flexibility they need to be quick and accurate as they encounter math in their lives.

When the students have become fluent at bundling and unbundling the sticks and at naming and writing the corresponding numbers, they are ready to switch to materials that require trading in. There are many commercial materials that are very good for working on these skills. Multibase arithmetic blocks allow students to see the relationships in a spatially consistent form. These blocks come from a variety of companies and might be called by the company name (e.g., Cuisenaire), but they are virtually always identified as materials useful for teaching place value.

Counting from 20 to 29

When the students are fluent on the numbers from 1 through 19, I begin working on 20 through 29. Once they have learned that *twenty* stands for *two* tens, this goes quite quickly. Students with disabilities, however, often don't become fluent for quite some time after they clearly understand the concept. The fast oral practice is especially important for these students.

I have taught this using the counting sticks with place value folders and using just the counting chart. Neither way seems to be better overall than the other way. If you use the counting sticks, you have to keep going back and forth from the counting sticks to the written numbers, which is a problem for some students who can't easily go back and forth between tasks. If you use just the counting chart, you must have the students very adept at thinking about bundling and unbundling tens because they won't have the sticks to bundle and unbundle. Since I make sure my students are very adept at that, using just the counting chart seems quite easy to me. I then have them work with the counting sticks and place value charts as soon as they can name and write the numbers automatically.

Materials needed besides pencils and paper:

- A counting chart that has 0 through 19 filled in on the first two rows and a blank row for the 20s.

Display the counting chart. Tell the students you will be working on the numbers that come after 19. Then ask them to review the ones and tens by saying something like:

> Let's look at the first row. We have all ones, don't we? We start with *zero* ones (point to each number as you describe it), then we have *one* one, then we have *two* ones, then *three*, then *four*, then *five, six, seven, eight*, and *nine*. Do we ever have enough to bundle in a ten? (*"No."*)

> Let's look at this row. (Point to the 10s row.) The next number after *nine* is *ten*. (Point.) Can we bundle ten ones? (*"Yes."*)

Yes, we can bundle ten, so we have *one* ten and *zero* ones. How about *eleven*? What can we bundle in *eleven*? (*"ten ones"*)

We can bundle ten ones, so we have *one* ten and *one* one. In *twelve* we have *one* ten and *two* ones. In *thirteen* we have *one* ten and *three* ones. In each number in this row (pointing across the row), how many tens do we have? (*"one"*)

So, when we get to *nineteen* we have *one* ten and *nine* ones. If we add *one* more one, what do we have? Most students will say *"one ten and ten ones"*, though some will immediately say *"two tens"*.

If you have some students who say *"one ten and ten ones"* and some who say *"two tens"* (or if they all say *"one ten and ten ones"*) tell them that they are right, but in order to write it in the next space we have to bundle the ten ones, so we have *two* tens. Write in the 2. Ask how many ones are left over and write in the 0. If all the students say *"two tens"*, just write in the 2 and continue asking about the ones.

To introduce the name, say something like:

Now we have *two* tens and *zero* ones. We call that *twenty*. *Twen ty* stands for *two* tens. We don't say anything for the *zero* ones, just like we only say *ten* for *one* ten and *zero* ones (point).

Write *twen ty* on the board and say *two tens* as you arc under the syllables of *twen ty*. Then arc again while you say *twen ty*.

Arc again while saying, If *twen ty* stands for *two* tens, which part stands for *two*? (*"twen"*)

Which part stands for tens? (*"ty"*)

I often say the same thing slowly a couple of times to give the students who process slowly more time to think. Write *two* and *tens* under the *twen* and *ty* to make it more apparent.

If someone comments on the similarity of the spelling or sound of *twelve* and *twenty*, reinforce their good observation; underline the *twel* and the *twen* and have the students say those parts of the words a couple of times. If no one comments on it, wait until you have finished introducing the 20s and then help them see the commonality in the names.

Go on to 21 by saying something like:

If we start with *two* tens and *zero* ones (point to the 20) and add *one* more one, we'll have *two* tens and how many ones? (*"one"*)

So I'll write the 2 for the *two* tens and I'll write a 1 for the *one* one. We call this *twenty-one*. Point to the numerals as you say the number.

In *twenty one*, what word stands for the *two* tens? (*"twenty"*)

What word stands for the *one*? (*"one"*)

What number do you think will come next?

Point below the next spot to let them see everything that is already filled in. If some students say *"twenty-two"*, tell them they are right and ask how they figured it out. If their explanations are right, confirm that and reiterate. If no one knows, if the explanations are wrong, or if they can't explain, use the same procedure used to teach 21. Then see if they can tell you what will come next (after 22). (If I am quite sure that no one will come up with 22, I don't ask; I go through the teaching procedure and wait until 23 to ask if they can come up with it.)

Be sure that any explanation for a number is clear to everyone before moving on to the next number. Some students will begin to see the visual pattern and can say the next number but can't explain how many ones and tens there are in the number. Until **each** of your students can explain the number in terms of ones and tens and can tell you that *twenty* stands for *two* tens, you must keep working on the verbalization of the concepts.

 Fast Oral Practice: Point to a number (e.g., 24) and ask them which number tells how many tens and which number tells how many ones. Ask for the tens and ones in random order. Ask what word we use for *two* tens. Ask which part of *twenty* stands for *two* and which part stands for the tens, or which part stands for the tens and which part stands for *two*, in random order.

Review the name for *ten* in the *teen* numbers by saying something like:

> Look here at *twenty-six*. (Point.) We've just said that the word *twenty* stands for the *two* tens in *twenty-six*.
> Look up here at *sixteen*. (Point.) What part of the word did we say stands for the ten in *sixteen*? (*"teen"*)
> So we use *teen* for one ten but *twenty* for two tens.

If someone comments that the *-teen* is backwards from the *twenty-*, reinforce the good observation. Tell them that for everything except the *teen* numbers we read from left to right. The *teen* numbers are backwards. At this stage, don't do anything else with this knowledge. When you finish the numbers through 99, come back to this idea and practice 13 versus 31, 14 versus 41, etc.

Writing Numerals and Number Words: Dictate numbers, sometimes calling them *twenty-__* and sometimes calling them *two tens and __ ones*, and have the students write them.

Have students write out the names for numbers by giving them four or five numbers on a paper and having them write: "*twenty, twenty-four, twenty-eight,*" for example. Also give them a sheet that has problems such as:

> *two tens* are _____ _____ (They write *twen ty*.)
>
> 24 is _____ *ty* _____

and so forth. This helps them get fluent at thinking what the words and the separate parts of the words mean, as well as making the spelling automatic. (Be sure that everything is spelled correctly.)

Working with the Place Value Chart

Materials needed besides pencils and paper:

- for each student, the ones and tens folder that you used for the numbers 10–19;

- about 30 counting sticks and a few bands for each student;

- the place value chart for you to write on;

- if your students cannot write relatively fluently, sets of word cards for them to represent the problems in a variety of ways:

    | two | | tens | | ten | | twenty | | one | | and | | fourteen | | nine | | ones | etc.

When your students can name and recognize the numbers up to 29, have them work with the counting sticks and their place value charts. Although they will be doing concrete representations of regrouping, the emphasis should be on the names of the numbers and on when they bundle and unbundle the sticks. **Do not** have them write any representations of regrouping at this point. That will come naturally when they are very fluent at representing numbers in varying bundles of tens.

If your students are using the word cards rather than writing the words, you might want to do the same. Put pieces of magnetic tape on the back of some of the cards and use a metal backed board or a cake pan to demonstrate the problems, rather than writing them. Have everyone write the numerals, though. That is part of what the students need to learn to do.

Do problems such as the following:

> Show me *two* tens and *six* ones with your sticks. Write the number 26 to the left of the tens|ones chart, as shown in Display 3-1.
>
> Good. To write that as tens and ones I write the 2 in the tens column and the 6 in the ones column. Let's represent it with words. What words shall I use? (*"two, tens, and, six, (and) ones"*)
>
> Good. I'll write (put) them over here. Write it or put the words to the right of the tens|ones chart.
>
> What other words can we use to describe this number? (*"twenty-six"*)
>
> Good. I'll write (put) them here.

Write it or put the words just below the previous words, lining up *twen* with *two*, the *ty* with *tens*, etc. Of course, if the students say *twenty-six* first, do that first and then elicit the *two tens*, etc. Have them explain why we can write it both ways. The explanation should include something about *twenty* meaning *two tens*.

Next, have them unbundle one of the tens into ones and describe how many tens and ones they then have. Write it in words next to the tens|ones chart. Show them that you can't write it on the chart on one line because you can't put 16 under the ones. Ask them how many bundles of ten they have (one) and put the 1 under the tens column. Ask them what you put in the ones column when

	tens	ones	
26	2	6	two tens and six ones *or*
			twen ty – six ones
	1	0	one ten (and)
	1	6	sixteen ones
	1	0	one ten (and)
	1	0	one ten (and)
		6	six ones

Display 3-1

you write the number *ten*. (0) Then ask them how you should write the 16 on the chart. Write that just below the 1 you already have in the ones column. If a student comments that the two ones can be added to make 2 and 0 and 6 make 6, so it's the same as it is above, confirm that this is right; it's just different ways of writing the same number.

See if anyone can think of a third way to write the number (1 ten and 1 ten and 6 ones). If no one suggests it, write (or put) *one ten* and *one ten* and *six ones*, and below that write (or put) 10 and 10 and 6.

Repeat these activities with two or three other numbers in the 20s. Be sure each student can name them in at least two ways and can tell you that we bundle when we have ten ones and, if we unbundle, we have ten more ones.

Fast Oral Practice:

- Point to a number (e.g., 25) and ask them which number tells how many tens and which number tells how many ones. Ask for the tens and ones in random order. Practice the same activity when you say the number instead of writing it.

- Have the students tell you how many ones they can bundle into tens in numbers that you show and say: Point to or say a number, such as 28, and say, I have *twenty-eight* ones. How many ones can I bundle into tens? (*"twenty"* or *"two bundles of ten"*) Elicit both answers. How many ones are left over if I make *two* bundles of ten? (*"eight"*)

- Have the students tell you how many ones there are in numbers you show or say. For instance, point to 23, and say, I have *two* tens and *three* ones. If I unbundle the tens, how many ones do I have altogether? (*"twenty-three"*)

- Ask what word we use for *two* tens. Ask, in random order, which part of *twenty* stands for *two* and which part stands for the tens, or which part stands for the tens and which part stands for *two*.

Writing Numerals and Number Words: If your students need the review, do again the writing activity described on page 19.

Also use a tens|ones chart like the one in Display 3-1 and have them write out the words to the right. At first you might have to say each word aloud before they begin writing. Nevertheless, they need to be able to describe the numbers using these verbal labels, so they should be able to write them, too, or choose the correct word cards if they can't write.

From 30 to 39

The teaching procedure is essentially the same as that for the numbers 20 through 29. One change, of course, is the name *thirty*; the other is that the students will bundle *thirty* ones into *three* tens. Again, this is described using just the counting chart but you could also have the students work with their counting sticks and place value folders while you do this.

Materials needed besides pencils and paper:

- A counting chart that has 0 through 29 filled in on the first three rows and a blank row for the 30s.

Display the counting chart. Tell the students you will be working on the numbers that come after 29. Then ask them to review the 20s by saying something like:

> Let's look at the numbers we just finished. We have (pointing) *twenty, twenty-one, twenty-two, twenty-three, twenty-four, twenty-five, twenty-six, twenty-seven, twenty-eight,* and *twenty-nine.* How many bundles of ten did we have in each of these numbers? (*"two"*)

> Right. We bundled *twenty* ones into *two* tens. If I add one more *one* to this *nine* (point to the 9 in 29) what will I have to do to the *ten* ones? (*"Bundle them."*)

> Yes, I have to bundle them. So now how many bundles of ten will I have? (*"three"*)

> (If necessary, add: I had *two* bundles of ten in *twenty-nine* and I just bundled another ten, so how many bundles of ten do I have? Unless you have a student who really can't keep track of more than one sentence at a time, you shouldn't have to do this.)

When your students say that you have three bundles, respond, Good; we have *three* bundles of ten. I'll write in the 3 on our chart. Write it just below the 20 on the counting chart, as in Display 4-1.

	1	2	3	4	5	6	7	8	9
10	11	12	13	14	15	16	17	18	19
20	21	22	23	24	25	26	27	28	29
3									

Display 4-1

We added *one* one to *twenty-nine*, so, instead of *nine* ones, we had *ten* ones. We had to bundle the *ten* ones, so how many ones do we have left over? (*"zero/none"*)

Good. We have *zero* ones. I'll write the 0 next to the 3. Write it in on the counting chart.

Now we have *three* tens and *zero* ones. We call that *thirty*. Write the word on the board and have your students say "thirty" a few times while you arc under the syllables as they say them.

In *thir ty* (arc under the syllables as you say them slowly), which part (syllable) stands for *three*? (*"thir"*)

Good. Which part stands for tens? (*"ty"*) If your students can't answer automatically, go back to *twen ty* and ask the questions.

Next, point to the place for 31 on the counting chart and ask if someone can tell you what the next number is, following the same procedures as you used for working on the 20s. Continue through 39.

 Fast Oral Practice: Point to a number (e.g., 35) and ask them which number tells how many tens and which number tells how many ones. Ask for the tens and ones in random order. Practice the same activity when you say the number instead of writing it.

Have the students tell you how many ones they can bundle into tens in numbers you say and show. For instance, Point to 38 and say, I have *thirty-eight* ones. How many ones can I bundle into tens? (*"thirty"* or *"three bundles of ten"*) Elicit both answers. How many ones are left over if I make *three* bundles of ten? (*"eight"*)

Have the students tell you how many ones there are in the numbers you say and show. For instance, point to 33, and say, I have *three* tens and *three* ones. If I unbundle the tens, how many ones do I have altogether? (*"thirty-three"*)

Ask what word we use for *three* tens. Ask which part of *thirty* stands for *three* and which part stands for the tens, or which part stands for the tens and which part stands for *three*, asking in random order.

If no one points out the similarity between the words *thirteen* and *thirty*, write *thir teen* on the board and write *thir ty* below it. Say something like, When we counted up from *ten*, we counted *ten, eleven, twelve, thirteen.* Say *thir teen* by syllables while arcing under the syllables. The name for *three* in *thirteen* is *thir.* The name for the *three* tens in *thirty* is *thir.* Say *thir ty* by syllables while arcing under the syllables.

Writing Numerals and Number Words: Dictate numbers, sometimes calling them *thirty-*____ and sometimes calling them *three tens and* ____ *ones*, and have the students write them. Give them four or five numbers on a paper and have them write *thirty, thirty-four, thirty-eight*, etc. Also give them a sheet that has problems such as: *three tens are* ____ __ (they write *thir ty*); 34 is ____ *ty* ____; etc. This helps them get fluent at thinking what the words and the separate parts of the words mean, as well as making the spelling automatic. Be sure that everything is spelled correctly.

Also use a tens|ones chart and have them write the words out to the right. At first you might have to say each word aloud before they begin writing. Nevertheless, they need to be able to describe the numbers using these verbal labels, so they should be able to write them, as well, or to choose the correct word cards if they can't write.

Working with the Place Value Chart

Materials needed besides pencils and paper:

- for each student, the *ones and tens* folder that you used for teaching the numbers 10–29;

- about 30 counting sticks and a few bands for each student;

- the place value chart for you to write on;

- if your students cannot write fairly fluently, sets of word cards for them to represent the problems in various ways. Add cards for working with the 30s.

Review the teaching procedures for 20 through 29. These will be the same, using 30 through 39. Do problems such as the following:

> Show me *three* tens and *six* ones with your sticks. (Write the number 36 to the left of the tens|ones chart, as in Display 4-2.)

> Good. To write that as tens and ones I write the 3 in the tens column and the 6 in the ones column. Let's represent it with words. What words shall I use? (*"three, tens, and, six, [and] ones"*)

> Good. I'll write (put) them over here. Write it or put the words to the right of the tens|ones chart.

> What other words can we use to describe this number? (*"thirty-six"*)

> Good. I'll write (put) them here. Write it or put the words right below the previous words, lining up *thir* with *three*, the *ty* with *tens*, etc.

> Of course, if the students say *thirty-six* first, do that first and then elicit the *three tens*, and so on.

Have the students explain why we can write it both ways. The explanation should include something about *thirty* meaning *three tens*.

Next, have them unbundle one of the tens into ones and describe how many tens and ones they then have. Write it in words next to the tens|ones chart. Show them that you can't write it on the chart on one line because you can't put 16 under the ones. Ask them how many bundles of 10 they have (two) and put the 2 under the tens column. Ask them what you put in the ones column when you write the number 10. (0) Then ask them how you should write the 16 on the

	tens	ones	
36	3	6	three tens and six ones *or*
			thir ty — six
	2	0	two tens (and)
	1	6	sixteen ones
	1	0	one ten (and)
	1	0	one ten (and)
	1	0	one ten (and)
		6	six ones

Display 4-2

chart. Write 16 just below the 2 you already have in the ones column. If a student comments that the *two* in the tens column and the *one* in the tens column can be added to make 3, and 0 and 6 make 6, so it's the same as it is above, confirm that. It's just different ways of writing the same number.

See if anyone can think of a third way to write the number (1 ten and 1 ten and 1 ten and 6 ones). If no one suggests it, write (or put) *one* ten and *one* ten and *one* ten and *six* ones.

Repeat these activities with two or three other numbers in the 30s. Be sure each student can name them in at least two ways and can tell you that we bundle when we have 10 and if we unbundle we have ten more ones.

Working in pairs or small groups, the students should be able to represent any number between 0 and 39 with counting sticks on their place value charts, showing the tens bundled and unbundled. They should also be able to represent the numbers in a variety of ways with their word cards or in writing. Finally, they should be able to describe them orally in a variety of ways.

From 40 to 99

At this stage, almost all students will be able to learn the names for the rest of the multiples of tens and count up from any of them. It is fine, however, to move through each set of tens (40 through 49, 50 through 59, etc.) just as you have gone through the 20s and 30s by adapting the directions in Chapters 2 and 3. Otherwise, work on the names of the multiples of ten.

Materials needed besides pencils and paper:

- a counting chart that has 0 through 39 filled in on the first three rows and spaces for the numbers through 99.

Display the chart and say something like:

> I think you could fill the rest of this chart in by yourselves. Let's review the pattern we've been using. Look up here at the ones. We get up to *nine* and then, if we add *one* we bundle the *ten ones* and have *one ten*. Point as you talk.
>
> Then we have a ten and we repeat all the ones. When we get up to *a ten and nine ones* and add one more *one*, we bundle *ten ones*, so we have *two tens*. So then we have *two* tens and we repeat all the ones.
>
> When we get up to *two tens and nine ones* and add one more *one*, we bundle *ten ones* so we have *three tens*. So then we have *three* tens and we repeat all the ones.
>
> When we get up to *three tens and nine ones* and add one more *one* we have to bundle the *ten ones*, so we have to write it over here. How many tens do we have now? (*"four"*)
>
> Good. We have *four* tens. Write in the 4.
>
> First we have *four* tens and *zero* ones, so I'll write in the 0. Then we have *four* tens (write in the 4) and *one* one (write in the 1).

What do I write in next? (*"a four and a two"*) Good. Write it in.

What's next? Keep writing in the numbers.

After you have written in 49, ask, **If I add *one* more one to *nine*, what do I have to do?** (*"bundle the ten"*) If the students jump ahead and want to write 5 (or 50) in the next space, acknowledge that they are right and ask them why. Elicit the knowledge that they had another ten so they had to go up one from the *four* tens to *five* tens and that you need to put in the 0 for the *zero* ones. After you have written in the 50, say something like:

> **If I have *five* tens here and keep counting up — *one*, *two*, *three*, *four*, *five*, *six*, *seven*, *eight*, *nine*, *ten* — how many tens will I have here?** Point to the spot for 60. (*"six"*)

> **Good. So I'll write in the *six* tens and add the 0 for *zero* ones.**

I count up quite fast, pointing to the spaces as I count. At *nine* I slow way down, and bring my finger back over to the tens (60) spot as I say *ten* and ask how many tens I have.

> **Now I have *six* tens and can just keep adding ones — *one*, *two*, *three*, *four*, *five*, *six*, *seven*, *eight*, *nine*, *ten*. How many tens will I have here?** Point to the spot for 70. (*"seven"*)

> **Good. So I'll write in the *seven* tens and add the 0 for *zero* ones.**

> **Now I have *seven* tens and can just keep adding ones — *one*, *two*, *three*, *four*, *five*, *six*, *seven*, *eight*, *nine*, *ten*. How many tens will I have here?** Point to the spot for 80. (*"eight"*)

> **Good. So I'll write in the *eight* tens and add the 0 for *zero* ones.**

> **Now I have *eight* tens and can just keep adding ones — *one*, *two*, *three*, *four*, *five*, *six*, *seven*, *eight*, *nine*, *ten*. How many tens will I have here?** Point to the spot for 90. (*"nine"*)

> **Good. So I'll write in the *nine* tens and add the 0 for *zero* ones.**

> **Now I have *nine* tens and can just keep adding ones. I'm going to write them in this time:** (Write as you say them.) ***nine* tens and *one* one, *nine* tens and *two* ones, *nine* tens and *three* ones, *nine* tens and *four***

ones, *nine* tens and *five* ones, *nine* tens and *six* ones, *nine* tens and *seven* ones, *nine* tens and *eight* ones, *nine* tens and *nine* ones.

Let's go back and look at the tens. Point to the spots for the tens as you describe them. We don't have any tens to start with. Then we have *one* ten, then *two* tens, then *three* tens, then *four* tens, then *five* tens, then *six* tens, then *seven* tens, then *eight* tens, then *nine* tens.

Now let's work on the names we use when we count. What do we call *two* tens? (*"twenty"*)

Good. What part of the word *twen ty* stands for *two*? (*"twen"*)

And what part stands for *tens*? (*"ty"*)

Good. What do we call *three* tens? (*"thirty"*)

Good. What part of the word *thir ty* stands for *three*? (*"thir"*)

And what part stands for *tens*? (*"ty"*)

Good. Now you can do the rest of these because they are the same as the names we use for the *teen* numbers.

	1	2	3	4	5	6	7	8	9
10	11	12	13	14	15	16	17	18	19
20	21	22	23	24	25	26	27	28	29
30	31	32	33	34	35	36	37	38	39
40									
50									
⋮									
80									
90	91	92	93	94	95	96	97	98	99

Display 5-1

Point to the *teen* number and then the *tens* number as you match them and ask the questions that follow (or draw arrows or lines from one number to the other, as pictured in Display 5-1). Develop the pattern like this:

> Just as we matched *thir teen* with *thir ty*, we'll match *four teen* with what?

If you get no correct response, say, while pointing to 30, *thir* stands for *three*, and *ty* stands for *ten*, and we have thirty. Here (point) we have four, and *ty* stands for *tens*. We have *for ty*, just as up here (point to 14) we have *fourteen*.

> How about the next one? Point to the 15 and 50 on the counting chart as you say,

> We match *thir teen* with *thir ty*, and *four teen* with *for ty*, so we'll match *fif teen* (write it next to *four teen* as you talk) with what? (*"fif ty"*).

> Good. *Fif ty. Fif* stands for *five* and *ty* stands for *tens. Fif ty.*

> How about the next one? Point to the 16 and 60 on the counting chart and then point to the words as you say,

> We match *thir teen* with *thir ty*, and *four teen* with *for ty*, and *fif teen* with *fif ty*, so we'll match *six teen* (write it next to *fif teen* as you talk) with what? (*"six ty"*)

> Good. *Six ty. Six* stands for *six*, and *ty* stands for *tens. Six ty.*

Repeat for 70, 80, and 90. Although it seems like you shouldn't need to keep going back to *thir teen* and *thir ty* each time, students who don't quickly master the language patterns benefit from hearing you say them over and over, and it doesn't hurt anyone else.

The touchy part of these comparisons is that we are still talking about *ones* in the *teens*, but in the *twenties* we are talking about how many *tens* we have. This part of the language that we use for counting in English is a real stumbling block for some students. Sometimes students reach the "Aha" moment with this idea while we are working through the next section or working with the counting sticks. Sometimes, though, that doesn't help, or a student is so confused that he can't follow the development of these ideas. In such cases I stop and work with the chart in Display 5-2. I add a *teens* column, write the words in syllables, and spend more time on the vocabulary that matches the work on the place value charts.

 Fast Oral Practice: You say ＿＿ tens and they tell you the number; you say the number and they tell you the tens. (They need to say "＿＿ tens," not just "five" or "six" or whatever the number is.) Also ask which part of *fifty*, for example, stands for *five* and which part stands for *tens*.

 Writing Numerals and Number Words: Say numbers and have the students write the numeral and write how many tens it has. (For instance, you say "sixty" and they write "60" and "6 tens.")

Reading and Writing the Number Names

Match up the number names by writing two columns, one for *ones* and one for *twenties*. Leave a bit of space between the syllables in the *tens* words. (See Display 5-2.) Point to the appropriate words while saying something like,

ones	tens
two	twen ty
three	thir ty
four	for ty
five	fif ty
six	six ty
seven	seven ty
eight	eigh ty
nine	nine ty

Display 5-2

> Let's look at the written names for the numbers. Here are the words for the *ones*, starting with *two* — *two, three, four, five, six, seven, eight,* and *nine*.
>
> Here are the words for the *tens*: *Twen ty*. How many tens are in *twenty*? ("*two*") And what part of the word stands for *ten*? ("*ty*") So we changed *two* to *twen* and added *ty* to say that we mean *tens*.

In *thir ty*, what part of the word stands for *three*? ("*thir*") What part stands for *tens*? ("*ty*") So we changed *three* to *thir* and added *ty* to say that we mean *tens*.

In *for ty*, what part of the word stands for *four*? ("*for*") What part stands for *tens*? ("*ty*")

Good. We have *four ones* and *four tens*. But look at what happens to
the spelling. We spell *four ones* as "f-o-u-r," but we spell *four tens* as
"f-o-r." It's not very nice of those folks who first wrote this down to
change the spelling, is it? Now we have to remember to write *four* as
f-o-u-r and *forty* as f-o-r before the t-y.

Continue with the rest of the words. Whenever you have an extra minute,
ask the students how many *tens* are in any one of the ten-multiple words, such as
seventy. Also have them write the number names for seatwork or homework, giving
them two or three at a time. Young children and students who haven't yet learned
to read words with *eigh* or *our*, or two syllables such as *seven* can match numbers
with their words and then trace the words. *Four* and *forty* will take extra practice
because they have the same sound.

Adding the *Ones* to the Counting Chart and Counting Chant

Using your previous counting chart on which you have filled in 40, 50, 60, etc.,
say something like:

> Now we're going to go back and fill in the rest of the *ones*. Look here
> at the 20's row. Point while talking.
>
> I have *twenty, twenty-one, twenty-two, twenty-three, twenty-four, twenty-*
> *five, twenty-six, twenty-seven, twenty-eight,* and *twenty-nine.* Then
> when we went up to *twenty* and *ten*, we bundled the *ten* ones and that
> made *thirty*.
>
> Let's say the *thirties* together while I point. Name the numbers through
> 39.
>
> When we go from *nine* (pointing to the 9 in 39) to *ten* (pointing off the
> chart next to 39) we bundle the *ten* and then we have (pointing to the
> 40) *forty*. Indicate that the students should say "forty" with you if they
> don't do it automatically.
>
> Let's say the *forties* together and I'll write them in.

Continue this way to 99.

 Fast Oral Practice: Say a number and have the students tell you
how many tens and how many ones you have. Tell them how many tens

and how many ones you have and have them tell you the number. Ask them how many ones you bundled in *fifty-five* (for example), and ask how many ones you have if you unbundle the tens in *seventy-six* (for example). These are the same activities as those listed for the 20s and 30s. Students need to be able to think this way automatically.

Have the students skip count by 10s. (See the general instructions for skip counting in Chapter 10.) When oral skip counting is fluent, have the students do one-minute speed drills writing the 10s.

Writing Numerals and Number Words: Say a number and have them write it. Say how many tens and ones you have and have them write the number. Give them a sheet with columns of _____ ones and _____ tens, with the ones or tens put first randomly; you say a number and they have to fill in the number of tens and ones.

This is usually a good time to look at the patterns on the counting chart to skip count by tens starting at any number (e.g., *twelve*, *twenty-two*, *thirty-two*, ...). Begin by looking at the first column (which has the tens and starts with *zero* ones). Say something like:

Let's look at the pattern of numbers on our counting chart. Let's start with this column. Point down the first column.

We start with *zero* ones. What do we do to get to this number? Point to 10. (*"We add ten."*)

Yes, we add *ten ones*, so we have to bundle them and we get *one* ten (point) and *zero* ones (point).

And then we add *ten* more, so we have *two* tens and *zero* ones.

I want the students to say at least the *"two* tens" with me. If you have developed a signal that tells them to say it with you, use it. If not, tell them to say it with you.

And then we add *ten* more, so we have *three* tens and *zero* ones.

And then we add *ten* more, so we have *four* tens and *zero* ones.

Keep going, saying everything except the number of tens quite fast and emphasize the number of tens so they hear the pattern of *one, two, three, four, five, six*, etc. Point to the number of tens each time. Sometimes students will observe that you could just keep going with *ten* tens and then *eleven* tens, and so on. Confirm that they are right and, if appropriate, count up orally with the students, saying the number and "tens" each time, through *twenty* tens. Stop at that point and tell them that they'll get to those numbers quite soon. Move on like this:

> Now let's look at the next column. Run your finger down the numbers.
>
> What's the only difference between this column (point to the first column) and this column (point to the second column)? (*"There were zero ones in the first column and there is one one in the second column."*)

It's very unusual for no one to suggest that, but if no one does, lead them to see it by comparing the tens in each column first by saying something like:

> Do we have any tens here? Point to the space before the zero. (*"no"*)
>
> Point to the space before the 1 and ask the same question.
>
> Point to the 1 before the 0 in 10 and ask, How many tens do we have here? (*"one"*)

Point to the 1 before the 1 in 11 and ask the same question. Repeat with 30 and 31, and 40 and 41. Then say,

> So, do the numbers have the same number of tens? (*"yes"*)
>
> Now look at the ones. How many ones did we have in this column? Point down the first column. (*"zero"*)
>
> And how many ones do we have in this column? Point down the second column. (*"one"*)
>
> So the tens stay the same but we have *one* one.
>
> Let's say the number of tens together. Here (point to the 1 [ten] in 11) we have *one* ten and *one* one. Here (point to the 2 in 21) we have *two* tens and *one* one.

Continue, emphasizing the number of tens and saying the rest quite quickly and with not as much emphasis. If someone wants to keep counting past the nine tens in 91, go on a little further.

Then practice the counting chants. It's harder for most students to start with the single digits or the *teens* because they sound different (e.g., *three, thirteen, twenty-three*, etc.), so I begin in the *twenties* for two or three examples first. Say something like, So if I say let's count by tens starting with *twenty-three*, we'll say *twenty-three, thirty-three, forty-three* .... Have the students say the numbers with you; point to the numbers on the counting chart while saying them. Have the students do one or two more examples like these, while you point to the counting chart and/or say the numbers with them, if necessary.

Practice the same counting chants beginning with the single-digit numbers. Say something like, Now we're going to do the same thing, but we'll start with *two*. Point to the numbers as you say them with the students, dropping out when you get up to the *twenties* or *thirties*. Repeat with one or two more examples.

Do two or three of these each day until the students are automatic. Have them write the sequences, also, doing them as speed drills if that gets them to work faster. When this is automatic, start at any number and have the students count up by tens (e.g., start at 44, or at 52).

Working with the Place Value Chart and Counting Sticks

Materials needed besides pencils and paper:

- for each student, the place value folder that you used for the numbers 10 – 39;

- about 100 counting sticks and a few bands for each pair or group of students;

- tens|ones charts for the students to write on;

- if your students cannot write relatively fluently, the sets of word cards for them to arrange to represent the problems in a variety of ways. Add the cards for working with the 40s through the 90s.

Have the students work in pairs or small groups, creating numbers with their counting sticks and writing those numbers in a variety of ways on their place value charts. Have them write (or use their word cards to create) the sentences that match what they have written. If they use their word cards, check periodically to see that they have used the right words.

		tens	ones	
	64	6	4	six tens and four ones *or* six ty – four
		6	0	six tens (and) *or* sixty (and)
			4	four ones four
		5	0	five tens (and)
		1	4	fourteen ones
		⋮	⋮	

Display 5-3

Display 5-3 uses 64 as an example to show the kinds of numbers and words your students should write. If they want to show all the tens separately with the 4 in the ones column at the end, that's fine, though it takes a lot of time so I usually have them do it for only one or two numbers. We'll talk about it orally for some more. Do this activity for several successive days until it is absolutely automatic for your students.

Comparing the *-teen* Numbers with 31, 41, 51, 61, 71, 81, and 91

When students reverse the digits for a number, these are the pairs they typically reverse. It makes sense because we say the *teen* numbers backwards compared to all the other numbers. I have found that many students will stop reversing the *teen* numbers if you merely explain that they are backwards. If you have introduced the numbers using these instructions, your students have already practiced identifying the *ten* and *ones* in the numbers, so some quick oral and writing practice is usually all they need.

If you have not used these instructions to introduce the numbers and place value, show the students that, except for the *teen* numbers, we always go from left to right, saying the numerals in the order they appear, and when we write the rest of the numbers, we write each numeral as we say it. For example, with 23, we name the tens first (*twenty*), then the ones (*three*). With the *teen* numbers we say the ones first and then the ten (*teen*). So when we write it, we write the 1 that stands for the ten (the *teen*) first, then write the ones. Until students are consciously aware of this and are automatic at saying and writing the numbers, they will often write them backwards.

 Fast Oral Practice: Say numbers (from 13 through 19 and the numbers listed above) and have the students tell you which part of the name they will write first. For example:

> For *thirteen* I'll write the *teen* first because it stands for the ten. What will I write first in *eighteen*? (*"the teen"*)
>
> Good. Why? (*"It stands for the ten."*)
>
> Good. In *fifty-eight* what will I write first? (*"fifty"*)
>
> Good. Why? (*"It stands for the five tens."*)

If students say only that it stands for the tens, ask them how many tens and tell them you want them to say how many tens. Continue, doing at least four of each in random order. Repeat this exercise for as many days as it takes for it to become automatic.

If your students are having trouble telling how many *tens* are in the numbers, you probably need to work through the activities described up to this point. You should be able to move through them quickly.

Writing Numerals and Number Words: Say these numbers and have the students write them. Do a speed drill on writing the numbers from 11 through 20 until the students are writing them at a minimum speed of three correct sets per minute. Have them say the numbers while they are writing them. This helps to connect the words with the kinesthetic memory of writing the numbers, as well as with what they look like. (Specific instructions for this appear in *Making Handwriting Flow*, Oxton House Publishers, 2001.)

Adding and Subtracting with Regrouping (Bundling)

It is now time to get the students fluent at adding sticks and taking them away when they have to bundle and unbundle tens and to represent what they are doing in writing, using the standard algorithm and notation for regrouping. (You can also continue teaching the numbers up from 99; see Chapters 6 and 7.)

Materials needed besides pencils and paper:

- the place value folder for each student;
- about 15 sticks, 10 bundles of 10 sticks, and a few bands for each pair or group of students;
- the tens|ones chart for you to write on;
- tens|ones charts for the students to write on;
- if your students cannot write relatively fluently, sets of word cards through the 90s for them to arrange to represent the problems in various ways.

Display the place value chart and ask the students to show you several examples of numbers with values between 40 and 99. Write some on the place value chart and have students write some, putting them in all the forms you've been practicing. Have the student un-bundle one of the bundles of 10 and

	tens	ones	
56	5	6	five tens and six ones *or* fif ty − six
	5	0	five tens (and) *or* fifty (and)
		6	six ones six
	4	0	four tens (and) *or* forty (and)
	1	6	sixteen ones sixteen ones

Display 6-1

write that, also. If they want to show a few numbers as individual tens, write those, too, but don't do any more than you think is necessary for solid development of the concept (because it takes so much time).

Begin working on regrouping by reviewing a couple of numbers, writing the results in two lines with the bundled tens on one line and the *teen* number on another. Then say something like:

> Today we're going to start working on the standard way of writing addition and subtraction problems when we have to bundle and unbundle tens. Let's start with adding. Here's the problem. I have *forty-six* books and I just ordered *seven* more. How many books will I have when the *seven* come? Write $46 + 7$ on the board as a horizontal problem.
>
> Show me the problem with your counting sticks. First show me *forty-six* and then show me *seven*. They should put *four* bundles of ten and *six* sticks on their folders, and then put *seven* more sticks on their folders.
>
> Good. Now how many sticks do you have in the ones? (*"thirteen"*)
>
> Good. What do you have to do with your ones? (*"Bundle ten of them."*) If they just say "bundle them," ask how many they bundle.
>
> Good. So you change the *thirteen* ones into *one* bundle of ten and how many ones? (*"three"*)
>
> How many tens do you have now? (*"five"*)
>
> And how many ones? (*"three"*)
>
> So how much is *forty-six plus seven*? (*"fifty-three"*) Add "= 53" to the right of $46 + 7$. Leave this on the board while you do the next activities.
>
> Now we need to figure out how to write what you did with your counting sticks. Start with showing me *forty-six* and *seven* again. (Pause while they do it.)
>
> Using your tens|ones chart, figure out how you could write what you do when you add those numbers.

Have the students work in twos or threes to come up with some way of recording what they have done as they combined the *six* sticks with the *seven* sticks, bundled ten of them and put the bundle with the other tens. If some of them are unable to even start, suggest that they begin by writing *forty-six* in a couple of different ways on their tens|ones chart to see which form might be the easiest to use.

You might need to remind them that whatever they write has to add up to *fifty-three*. If most of your groups have not represented all of the steps when they indicate they are done, you might want to tell them what they have not shown, or how their answer won't add up to 53 if they don't do something else.

When they have finished, ask each group to describe what they have written and how it matches what they did. If you have many groups, pick groups that represent different ways of doing the problems. Young students typically come up with examples such as in Displays 6-2 and 6-3.

tens	ones	
4	6̸	Some will write 40 below the 13 before writing the answer. Some will add another line below 13.
	7̸	
1	3	
5	3	

Display 6-2

tens	ones	
4	0	Some will write 13 and 40 below the problem and will then add them to get 53.
	6	
	7	
5	3	

Display 6-3

If they end up with results that aren't accurate (e.g., if they don't cross out the 6 and the 7 in the first example), show them what you would get for an answer if you leave it the way they wrote it. If your students are used to doing this within their groups, you can have a student do this. If all the methods result in a correct answer, remind them that mathematicians always look for the shortest, neatest way to write things. Of course, if a group has used the standard notation, point out how that conforms to the way mathematicians like to work and have the group that came up with it do a couple more examples, explaining what they are doing. Fix the explanation, if necessary.

Explaining the Standard Notation

For Addition

Write the problem on your tens|ones chart. Say something like:

First we add the ones. *Six* plus *seven* is *thirteen*.

We have to bundle *ten* of these and we have *three* ones left. Let's put the *three* ones in the answer spot. They're ones so they go here in the ones column. Write it in.

Now let's put that bundle of *ten* out of the way of the problem, but where we know we have to add it. Let's put it right above the *four* in the tens column. Write a 1 there.

Now we've taken care of the *thirteen* ones. We put the *one* ten above the *four* and the *three* ones in the answer spot.

Now we can add the tens. *Four* plus *one* is how many? (*"five"*)

Five. So I'll put the *five* in the answer spot. (Write it in.)

Review quickly: So when we have to bundle *ten* ones, we write the *one* bundle of ten above the tens in the problem (point) and put the ones in the answer spot. Then we add the tens and put that in the answer spot.

Do another problem (e.g., 58 + 24). Write the problem on the board while you say it. Have the students use their counting sticks to solve it and have them write the solution on their tens|ones chart. Let them write it in whatever way they can. This will tell you which students have internalized the standard notation and which haven't. If you have students who don't use standard notation but have gotten the correct answer, have them explain what they did. If their notation matches what they say, reinforce that and lead them through the steps to use the standard notation. Each student should be able to explain that we bundle *ten* ones so the *one ten* has to be written in the tens column.

Do three or four more problems; the students can make them up. It usually takes two to five days, doing four or five problems each day, for students to become quite good at this. Automaticity takes more practice, which can be done as seat work or homework as soon as students are accurate enough so that they won't make more than one random mistake for every five or so problems they do. Unless the mistake is on the regrouping, don't have them do more regrouping than they need in order to become fluent at it.

For Subtraction

To explain the standard notation for subtraction problems, say something like:

OK, now you can show what you do with the bundled ten when you add. We need to work on how you show unbundling. Here's a problem. I had *thirty-four* concert tickets to sell. I sold *eight* of them yesterday.

How many do I have left to sell? Write $34 - 8$ in horizontal form while you are saying the problem.

Use your counting sticks to show me *three* tens for *thirty* and *four* ones for *four*. (Students do that.)

Good, but now there's a problem. Do you have enough ones to take away *eight*? (*"no"*)

No, but how else can we show *thirty-four*? (*"two tens and fourteen ones"*)

Good. You can unbundle a ten and put the ones with the other ones so you have *fourteen* ones. Now take away the *eight* tickets I sold yesterday. (They do that.)

How many ones do you have left? (*"six"*)

And how many tens do you have? (*"two"*)

Good. So if you take *eight* away from *thirty-four*, what's left? (*"twenty-six"*) Write "= 26" to the right of your horizontal problem.

Now do the problem again and write down what you do on your tens|ones chart. Start by showing *thirty-four* with your counting sticks.

Have the students work in pairs or small groups, writing on their tens|ones chart what they are doing when they unbundle a ten and put the *ten* ones onto the ones folder. As with addition, point out any major flaws or remind them that the answer has to be *twenty-six*. If they have become fluent at writing 34 as 20 and 14, students will typically come up with something like Display 6-4. (Some of them may write 34 as 10, 10, 10, and 4.)

tens	ones
2	0
̸3	̸4
−	8
2	6

Some students will not cross out the 1 and 4. Sometimes they can't remember how they reasoned when they try to explain it later.

Display 6-4

After your students have finished, have them demonstrate what they did. Fix any problems and, if no one comes up with the standard notation, introduce it by reminding them that mathematicians always look for the shortest, neatest way to write things. Then say something like:

Instead of having to write *thirty-four* on two lines as *twenty* and *four-teen*, we want to be able to write *thirty-four* (write it in on your tens|ones chart) and then show it as *two* tens and *fourteen* ones all on the same line.

I'll cross out the *three* and write a *two* (2) above it (write it on the chart), and that will show the *two* tens.

To show the *fourteen*, I'll put a *one* (1) before the *four*, but up high enough so that I don't write on top of the *three*. That way I can read it. Write it in.

So now we have *two* tens and *fourteen* ones. Now I can subtract *eight* from the *fourteen* ones without taking up an extra line. Write in −8 on the chart.

Fourteen minus *eight* is *six*, which I'll write in the ones column.

And now I have *two* tens minus nothing in the tens column, so I'll just write *two* in the tens column.

Review that briefly: I unbundled a ten, so I wrote that beside the ones in the ones column. I crossed out the number in the tens column to show that I unbundled one of them and I wrote above it the number of tens I have left. Then I subtracted.

Let's do another one. Tim has *fifty-four* pens and is going to give Todd *nine* of them. How many pens will Tim have left? Write 54 − 9 in horizontal form on the board.

Use your counting sticks and your tens|ones chart to show me how to solve the problem.

Let them work in pairs or groups to describe what they do. Help any of them who need it. When they are finished, ask some of them to describe what they did. Be sure they explain the unbundling of a ten.

Do two or three more problems and then three to five problems each day until the students are accurate at the standard notation for regrouping and they all can explain why they unbundle a ten and how to show it in writing. When they become accurate at doing the problems, they can do a small number of problems for seat work or homework so that they become automatic at the process.

From 100 to 109

To learn the numbers in the hundreds, the students will bundle and unbundle *ten* of the bundles of ten. They need to learn to recognize, say, read, and spell the word "hundred" and also to recognize, say, read, and write numbers from 100 to 999. The bundling and unbundling process shows them how to write the numbers in hundreds and tens and ones, in tens and ones, and in ones. This understanding enables them to use the standard notation for regrouping in adding and subtracting.

You can add another folder to each previous place value folder by taping it to the left edge of the *tens* side. Tape it with a slight $\frac{1}{8}$-inch between the folders, taping on both sides so that the sticky part of the tape is completely covered. Display 7-1 shows the form of this double folder when open, with a panel left for *thousands*. If you cut about $\frac{1}{8}$-inch off the left edge of the new folder and the right edge of the old folder (on the *ones* side), when you fold in the sides and then "fold" the two halves together, the double folder will be the same size to store as the single one was.

tape

	hundreds	tens	ones

Display 7-1

It is difficult for some students to hold in mind information about three place values (including two sets of bundling), so I use the place value folders and three-column place value charts — I call them *hundreds|tens|ones charts* — along with the counting chart to develop the understanding of these numbers.

44

For numbers at least through 199, I have the students bundle *ten* bundles of tens for the *hundred*. The act of bundling emphasizes the renaming or regrouping at multiples of *ten*. Almost all students will be automatic at this by the time you have worked through developing the numbers from 100 to 199 and have added and subtracted using these numbers. Therefore, when I move from 199 to 200, I change from bundling *ten tens* to using a single counter to stand for a *hundred*.

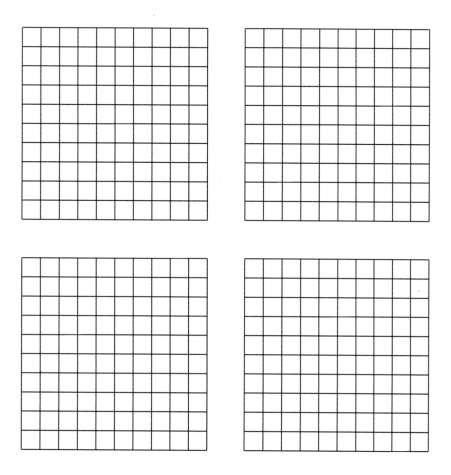

Display 7-2

You can use anything for the *hundred* counter that won't get confused with the single counters. I have used tongue depressors on which I write 100. (Of course, these should not be used if you have used tongue depressors for the *ones*.) If you are using pieces of paper for the counters, you can use a different color, being sure you write 100 on each piece. The material I like best is a square piece that has ten sets of ten squares. It's not only obvious that it's a *hundred*, it leads into multiplication well and also helps with understanding perimeters and areas. The counting materials such as Cuisenaire Rods or multibase blocks have these squares. You can also make grids on pieces of paper, laminating them if you want them to last for years. If you can't make them on a computer and print them out, you can photocopy the set of four in Display 7-2 as many times as you need.

If you have that unusual student with severe mathematical disabilities who does not become automatic at thinking in multiples of ten, continue having the student bundle *ten* bundles of *ten* for a *hundred* and unbundle a *hundred* into *ten* bundles of *ten* for naming the number by tens and ones.

Materials needed besides pencils and paper:

- the enlarged folder with the *hundreds* panel added;

- for each student, about 130 sticks or other counters, a dozen sleeves for bundles of *ten*, and a rubber band for a bundle of *ten tens*;

- the place value chart for you to write on, with the *hundreds* column added;

- place value charts for the students to write on, with the *hundreds* column added;

- the counting chart filled in through 99, with empty rows below that;

- if your students cannot write relatively fluently, the sets of word cards for them to arrange to represent the problems in a variety of ways. Add the cards for working with the *hundreds*.

One Hundred

Say something like:

> **You've become very fast and accurate when you are working with numbers up to** *ninety-nine*. **Today we're going to start working on the** *hundreds*. Write "hundred" on the board.

> **Look up here and say it with me.** Arc under the syllables as you say the word a few times.

> **Which letters spell** *hun*? (*"h-u-n"*)

> **And which letters spell** *dred*? (*"d-r-e-d"*) Repeat the word, arcing under the syllables.

Call their attention to their folders and how you've added to them and written the word on the panel to the left of the tens panel. If your students do not have many bundles of ten made up, have them make up eleven or twelve. They'll need only ten, but I've found that it's better to have more so that they have to count out ten, rather than just taking all of them. Display the counting chart (or just part of it) with the numbers up to 99 showing. Ask them to show you the number 98 with their counting sticks and write it on your hundreds|tens|ones chart. Have them add one to their sticks and write 99 on your chart. Ask them to add another one and ask them how many ones they have. If no one volunteers that they have to bundle the ones, ask them what they have to do when they get *ten* ones.

When they have bundled the ones and put the bundle with the other tens bundles, ask them to count the bundles of ten. They should have *ten*. If no one spontaneously says that they have to bundle them, ask them what they have to do when they get *ten*. Have them bundle the ten bundles and move it onto the *hundreds* panel. Then call their attention to your hundreds|tens|ones chart and ask them how many ones they have (*zero*), how many tens they have (*zero*), and how many hundreds they have (*one*). Write it on the chart as you go through them. At this stage I write the numbers evenly spaced in the center of the columns, as in Display 7-3. Students are comfortable enough with numbers so that the large spaces do not bother them.

Quickly review the word *hundred*, and have them write the word (or trace it). Ask what word we use when we bundle *ten* tens.

hundreds	tens	ones	
1	0	0	one hundred and zero tens and zero ones

Display 7-3

In words, write the number as tens and ones (just as you wrote the number *ten* as *ten ones* or *one ten*). Pointing to the number on your hundreds|tens|ones chart, say something like:

We said that this is *one* hundred, *zero* tens, and *zero* ones. I'll write that out here. (See Display 7-4.)

hundreds	tens	ones	
1	0	0	one hundred & zero tens & zero ones
			or ten tens & zero ones
			or one hundred ones

Display 7-4

What would I say if I wanted to name it by tens and ones? If I unbundle the hundred, how many tens is it? (*"ten"*)

Good; it's ten tens,... and how many ones? (*"zero"*) Write it out.

And if I unbundle all those tens, how many ones is it? (*"one hundred"*) Write it out.

Sometimes it helps to underline the 1 and 0 of the 10 tens while you ask for that name (*ten* tens and *zero* ones). Likewise, you can underline all three numbers when you ask for the ones. Students who are easily confused by charts and other visual diagrams may need to have you write the number three times for them to connect the underlined number with the words. Display 7-5 shows that.

Drawing their attention to the counting chart, point to 99 and ask how many ones there are in 99, and then how many tens there are. Ask what happened when they added a *one*, and then what happened when they put the bundled ones in the tens panel. Summarize that you have *zero* ones (writing in the 0), *zero* tens (writing in the 0), and *one* hundred (writing in the 1). Line them up so that the one hundred

hundreds	tens	ones	
1	0	0	one hundred & zero tens & zero ones
1	0	0	*or* ten tens & zero ones
1	0	0	*or* one hundred ones

Display 7-5

is in its own column. Compare this with the counting sticks the students have on their place value folders and with what you have written on the hundreds|tens|ones chart.

 Fast Oral Practice: Quickly review bundling and unbundling by tens by saying something like:

> How many ones do we bundle to put in the tens? (*"ten"*)
> How many tens do we bundle to put in the hundreds? (*"ten"*)
> If we unbundle a ten, how many ones does it make? (*"ten"*)
> If we unbundle *one* hundred, how many tens does it make? (*"ten"*)
> Good. So we always bundle or unbundle how many? (*"ten"*)

If a student says that we unbundle a hundred to make ones, confirm that we do this eventually, but ask if they get ones when they unbundle the hundred or when they unbundle the tens. You might need to do the physical unbundling while you ask the question for a student who processes language very slowly, but most students will "see" it in their minds if you ask them to visualize what happens.

101 to 109

Developing the numbers 101 to 109 in both oral and written language takes quite a bit of time with many students and should not be rushed. You will need to use their counting sticks, place value folders, and hundreds|tens|ones charts, along with your hundreds|tens|ones chart.

Ask the students to show you *one hundred* on their place value folder. Write it on your chart and have them write it on their charts. Ask them to add *one one* and to write the number on their hundreds|tens|ones chart. Write it on your chart. Ask them to describe the number to you in hundreds, tens, and ones. If anyone has written it wrong, having them say *"one* hundred, *zero* tens, *one* one" should lead them to fix it. If anyone still has it wrong, go through it one place value panel at a time, having them write the numeral in the chart as they describe what's in each panel. (Very few students write it wrong when they have put the counting sticks on their folders.) Then tell them how we say the number: *one hundred one.* Many people say *one hundred and one*; that's OK, too.

I've heard some criticism of the latter by teachers who want the students to listen for the "and" as a clue to where to put a decimal point, in the same way as they say monetary amounts. While many people write "and" before the xx/100 on their personal checks, not everyone does. In either case, it is the xx/100 which signifies the cents (the hundredths). In speaking about money, virtually everyone says dollars *and* cents: five hundred dollars and forty-five cents, etc. I don't recall hearing anyone say "five hundred and forty-five" without being questioned about what they mean, though I do hear "five hundreds dollars, forty-five cents" (without the "and"), and we commonly say, for example, "three sixty-five" when referring to a price of $3.65.

Whether or not "and" is used to indicate the decimal point, we need to specify what the *value* of the decimal place is: e.g., *fifteen and four tenths*, or *five hundred thirty-eight and three hundredths.* Without specifying what the decimal part is, there would be no way of knowing that the *four* means tenths or the *three* means hundredths in these two examples. My emphasis in teaching math skills always focuses on the concept and the language that matches that concept. Students need to become automatic enough with the words we speak so that they can respond correctly to the names of the decimal numbers. That way they will be able to communicate clearly with people who have learned different ways to name the whole numbers.

Write out the words for saying 101 as hundreds, tens, and ones, then as tens and ones, then as ones, using the hundreds|tens|ones chart as was done for 100 (above).

Proceed to 102 by asking the students to add another *one* to their place value folders. Ask them to write that number on their hundreds|tens|ones chart while you write it on yours. Describe the number in hundreds, tens, and ones, writing the words out as you do so. Have the students write (or choose) the words, also. Describe it in tens and ones, writing out the words. Finally, describe it in ones, writing out the words. Write it on the counting chart.

Proceed up the numbers, doing each step with each number through 109. In the first lesson, go as far as time and the focus of your students permits. Leave time for some fast oral practice and fast written practice with whatever numbers you have covered in each lesson.

 Fast Oral Practice: Point to a number (e.g., 104) and ask them which number tells how many hundreds, which number tells how many tens, and which number tells how many ones. Ask for the hundreds, tens, and ones in random order. Practice the same activity when you say the number instead of pointing to it.

Have the students tell you how many ones they can bundle into tens and into hundreds in numbers you say and show, as follows: Point to or say a number such as 103, and say,

> I have *one hundred three* ones. How many bundles of tens can I make? (*"ten bundles of ten"*)
>
> How many ones are left over? (*"three"*)
>
> How many bundles of a hundred can I make with the bundles of ten? (*"one"*)

Have the students tell you how many tens and ones there are in numbers you say and show, and then ask them to unbundle the tens, as follows:

> Point to a number such as 102, and say, I have *one hundred two* (or *one hundred and two*, if that is how many people in the students' community will say it). If I unbundle the hundred, what do I have? (*"ten tens and two ones"*)
>
> Be sure that the students tell you *ten* tens. If that isn't automatic, do three or four more examples before asking them to unbundle the tens.
>
> Good. Now if I unbundle the tens, how many ones do we have? (*"one hundred [and] two"*)

If students say "a hundred," instead of "one hundred," that's fine; just review that *a* means *one*.

If students get automatic at thinking of bundling ones into tens before bundling tens into hundreds, and unbundling hundreds into tens before unbundling tens into ones, even when there are zero tens, regrouping becomes essentially intuitive for almost all of them.

 Writing Numerals and Number Words: Dictate numbers, sometimes as *one hundred four* (for example) and sometimes as *one hundred, zero tens, and four ones,* and have the students write them in numerals. When the students are accurate at writing the numbers from 100 to 109, do speed drills on writing the numbers. Give them three or four numbers on a paper and have them write them in words, being sure that the spelling is correct (*"one hundred three"* etc.). Give them two numbers to write in words as hundreds, tens, and ones, as tens and ones, and as ones, as in Display 7-5.

From 110 to 199

Students should learn the numbers 110 through 999 fairly easily, but becoming automatic at naming them in a variety of ways needs practice. The biggest problem with the numbers 110 through 119 is that the *teens* are named backwards relative to the other numbers. If you have worked on this already (in Chapter 5), it will not be so hard now.

For many students, the larger problem at this stage is getting used to talking and thinking about *eleven* or *twelve* tens rather than thinking about those numbers only in relation to the ones. After developing the concept with the counting sticks and the hundreds|tens|ones chart, some fast oral and written practice will get them to be adept at it. Thinking about hundreds as tens makes regrouping almost intuitive and is crucial for understanding double-digit multiplication.

Materials needed besides pencils and paper:

- the enlarged folder with the *hundreds* panel added;

- at least 13 bundles of ten ones and at least 15 ones (more than needed for the problems), plus some rubber bands;

- the hundreds|tens|ones chart for you to write on;

- the hundreds|tens|ones charts for the students to write on;

- the counting chart filled in through 109, with empty rows below that;

- if your students cannot write relatively fluently, the sets of word cards for them to arrange to represent the problems in a variety of ways, including the cards for working with the hundreds.

One Hundred Ten

Introduce the new material by saying something like:

> Use your counting sticks to show me *one hundred nine* on your place value folder. They should have one bundle on the hundreds panel and nine ones on the ones panel.

> Now add another *one*. What do you have to do with the ones? (*"Bundle them and put the bundle on the tens panel."*) If anyone says only part of that (e.g., "bundle them"), ask questions to elicit all of it.

> Good; you bundled the *ten* ones into a ten and put it on the tens panel. Write the number on your chart. Write it on yours, also.

> How do you think we should say it? (*"one hundred ten"* or *"one hundred and ten"*)

It's unusual for no one to come up with the name, but if no one does, point to the 1 in the hundreds place and ask how they say that. Do the same for the ten. Then tell them the name while pointing to the numerals: So we have *one hundred ten*. If some students are confused about not saying anything for the ones, write 10 below the 110 on the hundreds|tens|ones chart and review the facts about its name: We say the ten but don't say anything for the *zero* ones. It also helps to draw a line under the 1 and 0, as in Display 8-1.

hundreds	tens	ones
1	1	0
	1	0

Display 8-1

> Now let's write the names for the number. If we name it in hundreds, tens, and ones, what should I write? (*"one hundred and one ten and zero ones"*) Write the words on your hundreds|tens|ones chart, as in Display 8-2.

hundreds	tens	ones	
1	1	0	one hundred & one ten & zero ones

Display 8-2

If I unbundle the hundred, how many more tens do I have? (*"ten"*)

Good. And how many tens do we have altogether? (*"eleven"*)

If someone says "eleven" in response to your first question, confirm that there are eleven altogether and ask how they got eleven. They need to be able to explain that ten of them came from unbundling the hundred.

So if I want to write it as tens and ones, what should I write? (*"eleven tens and zero ones"*) Write it on the chart.

If you need to, underline the 1 and 1 and cover up the word "hundreds" so that the eleven tens is visually apparent, as in Display 8-3.

	tens	ones	
1	1	0	one hundred & one ten & zero ones
			or eleven tens & zero ones

Display 8-3

Now if I unbundle the tens, how many ones will I have altogether? (*"one hundred ten"*) Write it on the chart, as in Display 8-4.

hundreds	tens	ones	
1	1	0	one hundred & one ten & zero ones
			or eleven tens & zero ones
			or one hundred ten ones

Display 8-4

If any students suggest that we can show it another way, ask them to show it with counting sticks and describe it. Usually they will keep the bundled hundred, but unbundle the ten and put it on the ones panel. That is perfectly fine. (In fact, it is what they will do when they regroup to subtract.) What is on the place value folder should be described as *one* hundred (and) *zero* tens (and) *ten* ones.

111 through 199

To introduce 111, repeat the activities for 110, beginning by having the students add one one to their place value folders. Do the same for 112 and 113.

This is usually a good time to use the counting chants practiced with the numbers up to 99 to explain the rest of the numbers without using the counting sticks. If you have developed automaticity on the counting chants through 109, you should not have to work with the counting sticks for each number. **However, if you feel that your students need to use their counting sticks to show each number up through 119, do that with them.** Then use the following procedures for developing the numbers from 120 through 199.

Move to the counting chart. Cover up the numbers below the 100 line with a blank chart and write in 110, 111, and 112. Point to the first column of numbers and say something like:

> Let's look at the tens in each of these columns. You've been counting by tens and we're going to do the same thing, but we're going to keep going past *one hundred.*
>
> First, how many ones are in each of the numbers in this column? Run your finger down all of the numbers in the first column. (*"zero (none)"*)
>
> Good. There are *zero* ones. Let's look at the tens. How many tens are in this number? Point to the number 1. (*"zero (or none)"*)
>
> How many tens are in this number? Point to 10. (*"one"*)
>
> How many tens? Point to 20. (*"two"*)
>
> How many tens? Point to 30. (*"three"*)
>
> How many tens? Point to 40. (*"four"*)
>
> Tens? Point to 50. (*"five"*)

Keep going, saying "tens?" quickly, so that what comes through is the counting from *zero* through *eleven.*

The next step is to write in the tens from 110 to at least 150 while the students say the number of tens. Say something like:

> Now I'll write in the next numbers as you say the number of tens, and I'll add the zero ones to each number. Let's start back here at the number *seventy.* (Point.) How many tens? (*"seven"*)
>
> Point to 80, etc. and say just "tens" quietly, so that the numbers are obvious.

When you get to 100 and 110, arc under 10 and 11, if necessary. Point to the spot for 120 when the students get there. If they readily say "twelve" write it in, arc under it, add the 0 for 120, and point to the spot for 130, continuing up to at least 150. If they don't readily say "twelve," remind them that they are adding one bundle of ten each time, so if there are *eleven* bundles and they add one bundle there are *twelve* bundles. If they add one more bundle there are 13 bundles. Continue to at least *fifteen* tens (150). If this was necessary, go back and count by the tens from 60 or 70, pointing to the numbers as you say the tens.

Move to the next column by saying something like:

> **Now let's look at the next column.** Run your finger down the numbers.
>
> **What's the only difference between this column** (point to the first column) **and this column** (point to the second column)? (*"There were zero ones in the first column and there is one one in the second column."*)
>
> It's very unusual for no one to suggest that, but if no one does, remind them by saying a few of the tens (*twenty, thirty, forty, fifty*) and then a few of the tens plus ones (*twenty-one, thirty-one, forty-one, fifty-one*), pointing while you say the numbers.
>
> **So the tens stay the same but we have *one* one. Let's say the number of tens together and I'll say the ones.** Point to the numbers as you say them. *One* ten and *one* one; *two* tens and *one* one.

Continue, emphasizing the number of tens and saying the rest quite quickly, with not as much emphasis. Arc under the 10 in 100 and the 11 in 110, if necessary. When the students say *twelve tens*, write it in and add the 1 for 121 as you say **and *one* one.**

Move to the next column, asking the students what changed (or what is different). Confirm that we now have *two* ones, but we still have *one* ten, then *two* tens, then *three* tens, etc. Repeat the procedure used for the previous column, saying, **one ten and *two* ones, *two* tens and *two* ones, *three* tens and *two* ones,** etc. When the students say *"twelve tens,"* write it in and add the 2 for 122 as you say **and *two* ones.**

If you think your students need it to really understand the pattern, continue looking at one or two more columns. If the pattern seems very apparent to all of your students, move on to looking at the rows.

Now let's look at the rows. Point as you talk, starting with the very first row.

We start here with *zero* and keep adding *one*. *One, two, three, four, five, six, seven, eight, nine,* and then we have *ten* and have to bundle them to make *one* ten.

Then we keep adding ones, so we have *eleven* (have them count with you), *twelve, thirteen, fourteen, fifteen, sixteen, seventeen, eighteen, nineteen,* and then what do we have? (*"twenty"*)

Keep counting together through 29 (or through 39, if you think your students will need it to focus on the pattern when you move to the hundreds).

Now skip to the 100 row and say something like:

When we got to *one hundred* we did the same thing. Let's count these. Point while you count, writing in the numbers not already there.

One hundred, one hundred one, one hundred two, one hundred three, . . . , one hundred ten, one hundred eleven, one hundred twelve, one hundred thirteen, . . . , one hundred twenty, one hundred twenty-one, one hundred twenty-two, one hundred twenty-three, . . . , through at least 139.

If your students are counting well and they need and want to continue, let them each say one of the sets of ten (140–149, 150–159, etc.), counting round-robin up to 199. You can write the numbers on the counting chart while they count, if you want to. If they go so fast that you can't keep up, write in the _8, _9, _0, _1 numbers. It's also good practice to have students take turns writing in numbers you haven't written in. If they can write the correct number in any spot you point to, with no help other than a reminder to look at the pattern, then they have the pattern pretty well internalized.

Whether you've gone through 139 or any other set of tens to 199, briefly review that we just start with *zero* ones and repeat all the numbers with *"one hundred"* before each number. Do the fast oral practice and writing practice with the numbers you have covered.

Fast Oral Practice: Point to a number (e.g., 124) and ask them which number tells how many hundreds, which number tells how many tens, and which number tells how many ones. Ask for the hundreds, tens, and ones in random order. Practice the same activity when you say the number instead of pointing to it.

Have the students tell you how many tens and ones there are in numbers you show, and then ask them to unbundle the tens. For example, point to the number 112 and say,

> I have *one hundred twelve*. If I unbundle the hundred, what do I have? (*"eleven tens and two ones"*)
>
> Be sure that the students tell you *eleven* tens. If that isn't automatic, do three or four more examples before asking them to unbundle the tens.
>
> Good. Now if I unbundle the tens, how many ones do we have? (*"one hundred twelve"*) If students say "a hundred" instead of "one hundred," that's OK, too.

If your students need to do the first example with the counting sticks, that's fine. However, if they need to continue using their counting sticks, they are not yet developing automaticity on the patterns in the counting chant and need to spend more time working with the counting sticks and the counting chart.

To unbundle hundreds from just hearing the number, rather than seeing it, students must be able to put the hundred together with the ten, which will be said as *twenty, thirty*, etc. This is difficult unless you can easily picture the number in your mind, so that you see the 11 in 116, the 12 in 124, the 13 in 138, etc. Young children and students who cannot visualize what has been said will not be able to do this without much, much practice. Since they will work mostly with written problems, this oral practice may not be necessary at this stage. You'll just need to be sure you always write a number you want them to rename in a variety of ways. However, it will be much harder for them to conceptualize quickly problems that are spoken, so they should get automatic at oral work before too long. Teaching them to "see" the number in their minds often helps.

Have the students tell you how many ones they can bundle into tens and into hundreds in numbers you show; e.g., point to 123 and say,

> I have *one hundred twenty-three*. How many bundles of tens can I make? (*"twelve bundles of ten"*)
>
> How many ones are left over? (*"three"*)
>
> How many bundles of a hundred can I make with the bundles of ten? (*"one"*)
>
> How many tens are left over? (*"two"*)

If this is too hard for your students, have them begin by showing the number with their counting sticks, but begin with the bundle of one hundred, the bundles of tens, and the ones. (Otherwise you have to wait for them to unbundle all of the sticks and then bundle them again.) Having to do this indicates that you need to spend more time representing numbers with the counting sticks, bundling and unbundling sets of ten while talking about the numbers in the variety of patterns possible.

 If you have a student who processes language very slowly, you'll have to decide if working more with the counting sticks on the place value folders is needed, or if you need to have more "wait" time after each question, repeating the question if the student requests it. As I suggested in the introduction, developing the language of mathematics is very important, but all of this language can be quite overwhelming to a child with a language processing problem and you may need to be very creative in developing ways of assessing when these students understand the concepts even if they can't respond spontaneously to your questions.

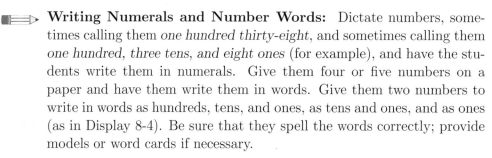 **Writing Numerals and Number Words:** Dictate numbers, sometimes calling them *one hundred thirty-eight*, and sometimes calling them *one hundred, three tens, and eight ones* (for example), and have the students write them in numerals. Give them four or five numbers on a paper and have them write them in words. Give them two numbers to write in words as hundreds, tens, and ones, as tens and ones, and as ones (as in Display 8-4). Be sure that they spell the words correctly; provide models or word cards if necessary.

If you did not complete the counting chart through 199, keep repeating the previous activities with the numbers through 199 until the students can do them fluently.

Count by tens up to 199, starting in a variety of places (e.g., 48, 69, 103, etc.). The hardest spot will be going from the 90s to the 120s (e.g., 92, 102, 112, 122), so be sure to have students say these patterns often. Point to the numbers on the counting chart if necessary. Do these orally and in writing. Do the same fast oral practice and writing exercises as you used for 100 – 139.

Regrouping with Numbers to 199

This should be a relatively easy continuation of the regrouping the students did with numbers below 100. The difference is in bundling tens to make a hundred or unbundling the hundred, instead of or in addition to bundling ones to make a ten or unbundling the ten. At this stage, the arithmetic problems vary considerably. One, two, or three digits can be added or subtracted, and there can be zeros in the ones and/or the tens place in the "top" number. The concepts are the same for all of the addition problems and for all of the subtraction problems, but some students need specific practice on each type, even if they understand the concepts. Here are typical examples of problems:

$$103 + 9 \qquad 146 + 7 \qquad 152 + 83 \qquad 160 + 150$$

$$103 - 8 \qquad 123 - 9 \qquad 103 - 35 \qquad 103 - 41 \qquad 135 - 68$$

The order in which you work on the problems doesn't really matter. You could work on all of the subtraction problems and then all the addition problems, or vice versa. You could work on problems like $103 + 9$ and then $103 - 8$, or $146 + 7$ and then $123 - 9$, etc., working on the same place value but alternating between addition and subtraction. These instructions start with addition.

Materials needed besides pencils and paper:

- the enlarged folder with the *hundreds* panel added;
- at least 200 counting sticks and 20 bands for each student;
- the hundreds|tens|ones chart for you to write on;
- the hundreds|tens|ones charts for the students to write on.

Addition

The addition process and, therefore, the questions to be asked, involve bundling ten of something (either ones or tens) and showing in writing what you have bundled. Say something like:

> You've been adding and subtracting when you have to bundle ones into tens or unbundle a ten to have ones. Now we're going to work on adding and subtracting when you have to bundle tens into a hundred and unbundle a hundred to have tens.

> Here's a problem. Tara has read *one hundred thirty-six* books for the book reading contest. She figures she has time to read *eight* more. How many books will she have read when the contest ends? Write $136 + 8 =$ in horizontal format on the board.

> Show me the problem with your counting sticks. Start with *one hundred thirty-six* and then add *eight*. What do you have to do? (*"Bundle ten ones and put the bundle on the tens folder."*)

> Good. So how many books will Tara have read? When they give the answer, write it on the board.

> Now write the problem on your place value chart, just like I'm doing. Write the problem in vertical format on your place value chart, as in Display 8-5.

> Now show what you did to solve the problem.

Be sure that they all show the carried number. When they have finished, ask someone to describe in words what they did. This is the same as what they did with numbers up to 99, except that they have to add the hundred. If anyone has trouble, cover up the 1 for the hundred in your example and ask them how they would solve the problem. Then ask how many hundreds they have altogether and ask them where they will write the hundred.

hundreds	tens	ones
1	3	6
+		8

Display 8-5

If you think your students need to solve some problems just with the counting sticks before writing any in standard notation, give them a few more problems to solve. You can back up and use the same problems when you ask them to write.

Here's another problem. It's 140 miles to Gram's. We're going there on Sunday. Monday afternoon we're going to Uncle Dean's. His house is 70 miles past Gram's. How many miles will we have gone by Monday evening? Write the problem on the board in horizontal format.

Show me the problem with your counting sticks. Put on 140 miles and then put on 70 miles.

After they have put the counting sticks on their folders, ask them to tell you what they will need to do to solve the problem. If they can't, ask them if they have to bundle any ones, and then if they have to bundle any tens. Have them do that. Ask what the answer is and write it on the board. Then have the students work on describing what they did and why (bundled *ten* tens to make a hundred because whenever you have ten of anything you have to bundle it). Have them write the problem on their place value charts and show what they did in standard notation.

If it appears that the students understand the concept of bundling and can use it correctly regardless of what numbers are in each place, give them three or four more problems to solve, describe, and write in standard notation. Help when necessary by referring to bundling and unbundling ten of whatever is necessary. Do three to five problems each day until the students are fluent at solving, describing, and writing the problems. Not all of the problems need to have stories attached; however, students are usually good at making up real-life stories themselves and can work in pairs or trios, giving each other problems to solve. I often give them the numbers and have them make up the stories.

Subtraction

The subtraction process and, therefore, the questions to be asked, involve unbundling a hundred or a ten (or both) and showing in writing what you have unbundled. Subtraction is a bit harder than addition because you often have to "borrow across" a zero, as in $103 - 8$. In such situations, many students think of unbundling a hundred as turning it into ten ones, instead of ten tens. Working with the counting sticks takes care of that problem.

It's usually easiest to begin by working on problems like $143 - 8$, and then like $154 - 63$. Use the same questions as those for developing the unbundling process with numbers below one hundred (pages 41–43). Do enough problems with the counting sticks to be sure that the students understand the concept. If they struggle with writing the numbers, do more fast oral and written practice (see pages 51–52).

The following instructions are for problems that require borrowing across the tens to the hundred. I find that many students need help with these problems. I have them show everything with their counting sticks until I am sure that they can write what they did correctly and easily. Some students will need to go back and forth from working with their counting sticks to writing what they did for each place value. Others can complete a problem with their counting sticks and then write what they did for the whole problem. Say something like:

> Now we're going to work on subtraction problems that start with *zero* tens. Here's a problem. Josie has 102 baseball cards and is going to give 4 to Yolanda. How many will Josie have left?
>
> Show me Josie's 102 cards with your counting sticks.

Write the problem on the board in horizontal form as you say it. When the students have represented 102 on their folders, say,

> Now you need to take Yolanda's *four* cards away. What do you have to do to have enough ones to take *four* away? (*"unbundle the hundred"*)

If no one suggests that, ask if they have any tens to unbundle and then move to the hundred. Have them unbundle the hundred and put the tens on the tens panel. If no one suggests unbundling one of the tens, ask them, **Now what can you unbundle?** Then ask how many ones they have, and have them take away *four* of them. Have them tell you the answer to the problem; write it on the board.

Review what they did by saying something like, **You didn't have enough ones to subtract (take away) *four*, so you had to unbundle something. You didn't have any tens to unbundle so you had to unbundle the hundred into tens, and then unbundle a ten into ones. Let's show that in writing. Write the problem on your place value chart. Write it on yours, as in Display 8-6.**

hundreds	tens	ones
1	0	2
−		4

Display 8-6

> How do we show that we unbundled the hundred? (*"Put a line through it"* or *"cross it out."*)
>
> Good. How many hundreds do we have? (*"none / zero"*) Write it in.
>
> How many tens do we have now? (*"ten"*)
>
> How do we show the *ten* tens? (*"Put a one before the zero to say ten."*)

> Can we take away *four* yet? (*"no"*)
>
> What do we have to do? (*"unbundle a ten"*)
>
> Good. We have to unbundle a ten and write it as ones. How do I show that? Tell me what to do with the tens first. (*"Cross out the ten and write nine above it."*)
>
> Now tell me where to write the *ten* ones. (*"Put a one before the five."*)
>
> Good. Now can we take away *four*? (*"yes"*)
>
> Good. So we unbundled a hundred and showed the tens by putting the *one* before the *zero*; then we unbundled a ten, so we had *nine* tens and *twelve* ones. Then we could take away *four*.

If you have students who can't remember what they did with their counters, have them redo each step of the problem and write it as they do it: (Show me Yolanda's 102 cards and write it on the place value chart; what do you have to unbundle and write that on the place value chart; now what can you unbundle; write that; etc.) These students usually need to do more problems with their counting sticks than students who can do the whole problem before writing it down.

> Here's another problem. The Rogers have 105 baby chickens. The Perrys want to buy 8 of them. How many will the Rogers have if they sell 8 to the Perrys? Write the problem on the board in horizontal form.
>
> Use counting sticks to show me how many baby chicks the Rogers have.

When they have 105 represented with counting sticks ask them to show you what they have to do to take 8 away. Most students will be able to complete the problem and describe what they did. If anyone can't, go through the questions from the previous problem. Write the answer on the board.

Have the students write the problem on their place value charts themselves, asking prompting questions, if necessary. If the students struggle with this, but are fluent with regrouping up to 99, you may need to spend more time renaming numbers on the place value chart and doing fast oral and written practice on naming the numbers as hundreds, tens, and ones. (See these activities on pages 51–52.)

Have the students do four or five problems of a variety of types each day until they are fluent at solving, describing, and writing the problems.

From 200 On

From 200 to 999

To keep going up the counting chant, you can begin with the counting sticks and the place value folders, you can begin with the place value chart, or you can begin with the counting chart. By this time, the students should be so fluent at thinking of the patterns that it really doesn't matter which way you start. Here is a list of the tasks that the students should be able to complete with any number from 200 through 999. These are the same activities that have been emphasized all along in this book. The order in which you practice them doesn't usually matter. A few students will do better if you always start with the counting sticks, but even those students should get fluent enough with the patterns for you to start with the counting chart if you want.

- Show any number with the counting sticks and the materials you use for representing hundreds.

- Write any number in numerals and in words (or choose the appropriate word cards).

- Write any number in numerals on the place value chart.

- Tell orally or in writing the number of hundreds, tens, and ones in any number you show them with counting sticks, or write, or dictate.

- Tell orally or in writing the number of hundreds and tens you would have if you unbundle one hundred in any number you show them with counting sticks, or write, or dictate.

- Tell orally or in writing the number of ones you would have if you unbundle the tens or the hundreds in any number you show with counting sticks, or write, or dictate.

- Describe the patterns in the numbers on the counting chart by columns and by rows (i.e., we repeat the ones from zero through 99 for each hundred; we repeat the tens from zero though nine for each hundred; we count tens from zero though 99 for the whole set of hundreds; we count ones from zero through 999 for the whole set of hundreds; we count hundreds from zero through 9 for the whole set of hundreds).

- Add and subtract any numbers through 999, using counting sticks, place value charts, or ordinary paper, and using standard notation as well as any other (correct) writing strategies the students might come up with.

Thousands

Two important, familiar patterns underlie teaching the thousands:

1. The pattern of bundling ten of the previous quantity (hundreds, then thousands, then ten thousands) continues, to make one of the next size each time (one thousand, then ten thousands, then hundred thousands).

2. The previous pattern of ones, tens, and hundreds repeats, but this time we count thousands instead of ones.

Add the word "thousands" to your students' place value folders and place value charts, and add it to your place value chart. You'll need something to represent a thousand for the counting folders. If you are using one of the commercial sets of materials such as Cuisenaire rods, they have cubes. If you are not, you can use a drawing of a cube like the one in Display 9-1, or a stack of ten of the hundreds squares clipped or taped together. Using a cube (in some form) is good for later work with powers. On the place value chart, I like to add *ones*, *tens*, and

Display 9-1

hundreds columns under the word "thousands" when I get to *ten thousand*. I like to have the added words on the same level as the previous *hundreds*, *tens*, and *ones* headings, so I write the word "thousands" a little higher on the chart, as in Display 9-2.

Introduce the word and write it on the board as you say it. Either space between the syllables (*thou sands*) or arc under the syllables after you have written it. Have the students say it with you a couple of times. Ask them to spell *thou* and *sands*, being sure you pronounce *sands* with the normal schwa sound. It helps some students with spelling if you then point out that if we pronounced that syllable as though it were a word by itself, it would say "sands" (often a student will point this out). Pronounce the word both ways. Have them write the word a couple of times.

Use the same teaching strategies used for the hundreds, beginning with having the students show you 999 with their counting sticks. Ask them to add *one*, so that they have to bundle the ones, which will result in *ten* tens, so that they have to bundle the tens, which will make *ten* hundreds, so that they have to bundle the hundreds, which will make a thousand. Write the thousand on the place value chart, calling it *one thousand*, or *ten hundreds*, etc., as in Display 9-2. Underline the numbers of hundreds, tens, and ones on the chart, covering the words also, if you need to.

thousands	hundreds	tens	ones	
1	0	0	0	one thousand & zero hundreds & zero tens & zero ones
1	0	0	0	*or* ten hundreds & zero tens & zero ones
1	0	0	0	*or* one hundred tens & zero ones
1	0	0	0	*or* one thousand ones

Display 9-2

Give the students several more numbers to write on their place value charts and describe as thousands, hundreds, tens, and ones, using any number of thousands. Have them show some of them on their place value folders.

Review bundling and unbundling several times, so that the pattern of tens is automatic. Do several addition and subtraction problems that require regrouping. All this should be relatively fluent, even when regrouping "over" zero tens and/or zero hundreds. If it is not, work more on bundling and unbundling, rewriting the numbers as you work. Be sure that the students can describe what they are doing.

At some point I usually have the students stack their counting materials up in a pattern to help emphasize the repetitions of tens. This takes considerable space. I have them put ten rows of ten counters with a ten to the left of each row. We put a piece of string or yarn below that. Below the tens, I have them stack up ten sets of tens with a *hundred* square to the left of each stack. Again, we put a piece of string or yarn below that. Below the hundreds, I have them stack up ten sets of hundreds with a *thousand* cube (or clipped set of hundreds) to the left of each stack. I like to go up to at least 3,000; go farther if you have the materials to do it. (Having students work in groups allows you to use everyone's materials.)

We then review that we repeated ones for each ten until we got to one hundred; then we repeated tens for each hundred until we got to one thousand. We go back and count by tens while I point to each ten as we say the number. Then we count the hundreds. Then we count the tens up to the thousand. Usually I have to remind them that we counted only one ten each time until we got to ten (the hundred), but then we had *ten* tens in each stack, so we have *eight, nine, ten,* and then *ten* more makes *twenty,* and *ten* more makes *thirty,* etc., to *one hundred* of them. I'll often then ask them how many ones they'd have to stack up for any of the numbers. This is just another way of emphasizing each number as ones, tens, hundreds, etc. It makes the quantities more concrete than they are on a place value chart that just has numbers.

Ten Thousand

Display 9-3

After you've worked with numbers up to 9,999, it's hard to use the place value folder because it's hard to "bundle" tens of the thousands. By this time your students should be so fluent at thinking about the numbers and place values that they shouldn't need the concrete materials. If you or your students want to use concrete materials, I suggest using a picture of ten cubes, as in Display 9-3 (which you can photocopy).

The pattern that should become automatic for the students is the repetition of the counting pattern, this time by thousands instead of by ones: *one thousand, two thousand, ..., ten thousand, eleven thousand, twelve thousand, ..., one hundred thousand, one hundred one thousand, ...* To make this more apparent visually, I add the words "hundreds, tens, ones" below "thousands" on the place value chart, as in Display 9-4.

Display 9-4

Here is the list of activities that the students should be able to do with fluency before you move on to the millions.

- Show any number with the counting sticks and the materials you use for representing hundreds and thousands.

- Write any number in numerals as well as in words (or choose the appropriate word cards).

- Write any number in numerals on the place value chart.

- Tell orally or in writing the number of thousands, hundreds, tens, and ones in any number you show with counting sticks, or write, or dictate.

- Tell orally or in writing the number of thousands, hundreds, and tens you would have if you unbundled one thousand in any number you show with counting sticks, or write, or dictate.

- Tell orally or in writing the number of ones you would have if you unbundle the tens, hundreds, or the thousands in any number you show with counting sticks, or write, or dictate.

- Add and subtract using any numbers through 999,999, using counting sticks, place value charts, or ordinary paper, and using standard notation, as well as any other (correct) writing strategies they might come up with.

Millions, Trillions, etc.

If it is appropriate for your students to continue with these larger numbers, use the place value charts to develop the pattern of bundling ten of the previous numbers. Practice the following activities:

- Write any number in numerals as well as in words (or choose the appropriate word cards).

- Write any number in numerals on the place value chart.

- Tell orally or in writing the number of millions, (trillions, etc.), thousands, hundreds, tens, and ones in any number you write. It's probably too hard for most students to do this if you just dictate numbers, unless you have them write the number before telling you the millions, etc.

- Tell orally or in writing the number of thousands, hundreds, and tens you would have if you unbundled one million (trillion, etc.) in any number you write.

- Tell orally or in writing the number of ones you would have if you unbundle the tens, hundreds, thousands, or millions (trillions, etc.) in any number you write.

- Add and subtract using any numbers through 999,999, using counting sticks, place value charts, or ordinary paper, and using standard notation as well as any other (correct) writing strategies they might come up with.

Skip Counting

Students should start doing counting chants other than *one, two, three, four, ...* as soon as they can count past 100. (With young children, you might want to do some of them as soon as they can count to 40 or 50, but it's usually more efficient to wait until they can count to 100.) This is often called **skip counting**. To be most beneficial, students should perform a variety of counting chants and practice them in a variety of ways. An early activity for any counting chant should involve visual displays of numbers to add another modality to their learning. I use the counting chart for the visual display. I like to use an overhead transparency and lay colored, transparent markers over the numbers to show the patterns.

It's helpful if the students each have a counting chart to use for practice on their own. The blackline master included as a foldout sheet at the end of this book makes charts that can be laminated and are big enough to be used by individual students or small groups working together. Small, translucent bingo chips allow the students to cover numbers but still see them, so that the patterns become clear visually. Use the chart as you practice each new counting chant, either covering the numbers with chips, or having the students point to the numbers as they say them.

Students should say the chants, or skip count out loud, practicing until they are fluent. Ideally, they should be able to start at any number in the chant and proceed up from there (e.g., 5, 10, 15, 20, 25, 30, ..., or 15, 20, 25, 30, 35,..., or 30, 35, 40,...). When the chants are fluent and students can easily point out the appropriate numbers on the counting chart, have them write the chants. Do this as a speed drill, either timing them for a certain length of time or recording how long it takes to write a particular chant. (Detailed instructions for this appear in the booklet, *Making Handwriting Flow*, Oxton House Publishers, 2001.) This chapter describes the chants that I typically practice, in an order that seems to be appropriate for most students. Change the order when it makes sense for what your students know and are working on.

The Tens

Counting by tens to 100 is usually the easiest chant after learning to count by ones. If you have used the approach in this book to teach the numbers and place value, your students should be doing this with no trouble. Introduce the activity by saying something like,

> We're going to count by numbers other than *one*. We call this "skip counting" because we skip the numbers in between the ones we are counting. We've been counting the tens. Let's say them together while I point. (*"ten, twenty, thirty, forty, fifty, sixty, seventy, eighty, ninety, one hundred, one hundred ten"*)

If students want to keep going, that's fine. The goal is to have them count by tens without looking at the chart, but let them look as long as they need to.

When the students are fluent verbally, have them write the chant as a speed drill. This is best done for 1 minute, recording the number of correctly written and sequenced items done in that minute. Be sure that students space between the numbers more than between the individual digits in the numbers. If your students can't write fast enough to get at least to 110 in a minute, either give them a longer time period or record the number of seconds it takes them to do the whole sequence up to 110. Since they will have written only 23 digits to get through 110, it should not be a problem. If they finish before the minute is up, have them continue up in the sequence if they can, or have them start over with 10. First graders may not get much more than one sequence finished in a minute, but by second grade most students should be able to write at least 50 digits in a minute, which would mean more than two sequences of 10 through 110, or well past 200 if they keep going beyond 110.

I expect the students to count up by tens from any number I give them. For example, if I say *twenty-two*, they have to count *"thirty-two, forty-two, fifty-two, sixty-two, ..."* up as high as they have been counting. Often, they need the chart when we begin doing this, but it should be automatic before long. With a large group, I will do some written one-minute speed drills with these to be sure that everyone is gaining fluency. Having the students do the skip counting orally together provides the most practice for everyone, but it doesn't allow you to monitor each student. The written speed drills do that.

These instructions work equally well for the other counting chants and should be used for them. The following sections do not repeat them in detail, focusing instead on useful differences in the counting patterns.

The Fives

Practicing the fives at least to 60 is usually next, and I have the students use chips to cover the numbers on the counting chart as they count. (Counting by fives to 60 is useful for learning to tell time.) Have the students point to the numbers on the counting chart as they count until they are fluent with the verbal chant. Count up from any "five" (e.g., 25, 30, 35, 40, ...; 70, 75, 80, 85, ...). Do written speed drills for how far up you counted (e.g. to 60, or as high as your students can go).

When I use this chant, we then discuss the fact that the numbers either end in 5 or else are a ten. I'll say numbers and they have to tell me if the number is a "counting by five" number. For example, I'll say *thirty* and they tell me it's a counting by five number because it's a *ten*. I'll say *forty-two* and they tell me it's not a counting by five number because it doesn't end in *five* and it's not a *ten*.

The Twos

Counting by twos for the even numbers is next, if not before the fives. I go as high as students can count by ones (but not higher than 150!). After covering the numbers on the counting chart, discuss the pattern, showing that you can start at any ten and repeat the same ones (*two, four, six, eight*). It often helps students become fluent at this if you say the tens and have them say the twos:

twenty *"two"*, twenty *"four"*, twenty *"six"*, ...

thirty *"two"*, thirty *"four"*, thirty *"six"*, ...

Again, start in different places and have them count up from there, and do appropriate written speed drills.

Although I don't have students count by twos for the odd numbers, I do teach them the terms *even* and *odd* and I do say numbers and have them tell me if the number is even or odd. We do this by deciding whether or not the number is even; if it is not, it's odd.

Larger Numbers

What you work on next depends on how high your students can count and on what other skills they are learning. If they are fluent with the patterns of hundreds to 1,000 and are learning money skills, it makes sense to count by 25. The counting chart doesn't help much with this, so write out a series of numbers starting with 25. I like to arrange them as in Display 10-1.

By this time, your students should be very fluent with thinking about the numbers of ones in various larger numbers. As soon as they can relate penny to *one*, a quarter to 25, and a dollar to 100, they can switch back and forth between numbers and pennies to describe these. Again, have them start anywhere and count up (e.g., *"one hundred twenty-five, one hundred fifty, ... "*, and *"one twenty-five, one fifty, one seventy-five, two dollars, ... "*), and do written speed drills.

	25	50	75
100	125	150	175
200	225	250	275
300	325	350	375
400	425	450	475
500	525	550	575
⋮	⋮	⋮	⋮

Display 10-1

It is also useful to count by 50s for estimating and for multiplying and dividing, but half-dollar coins are seldom used, so I don't connect this counting chant to coins. When students are fluent enough with money skills to bother with 50-cent pieces, they don't need to practice counting them. Many students will be able to skip count by 50s without a visual pattern. If they can't, have them write the fives chant with plenty of space between the numbers (or with the numbers on separate lines) and then, with a different color, go back and add the 0s to make 50, 100, 150, etc. After that, have them practice both counting chants (fives and fifties) as they point to the numbers.

Once students can count up several hundred, they can usually count by thousands as soon as they know the word "thousand." The same will be true for million, billion, etc. However, many students need practice on skip counting by large numbers when they do not start at a multiple of 10. Pick random numbers for them to start at and have them count up by hundreds, thousands, millions, etc. If you pick 550, for example, and have them count by hundreds, they will say *"five hundred fifty, six hundred fifty, seven hundred fifty,"* etc. If you pick 2,004 and have them count by thousands, they will say *"two thousand four"* (or *"... and four"*), *"three thousand four, four thousand four,"* etc. You might have to have them tell you which numbers will not change and which number will change. (*"The four will not change; only the two thousand will change."*)

Some students might need to have the numbers 1 through 9 where they can see them when they first start doing this, and you might have to point to the next number as they work. Explain that they can use the numbers to help themselves keep track of which thousand (or million, etc.) they are on. I will also have them say the number that changes and I'll add the number that doesn't. For example, they'll say *"two thousand"* and I'll say four (or and four); they'll say *"three thousand"* and I'll say four; etc.

The Threes and Fours

If your students are working on multiplication and division, adding the skip counting chants for threes and fours will give them a way of quickly calculating most problems and will make it easier for them to memorize the number facts.

Have them skip count by threes at least up to 30. On the counting chart, have them put chips on the numbers at least up to 60. This allows them to see the pattern visually, making the repetitions very apparent. Ask them to describe these patterns; if they can't, show them at least the repetition of the pattern from 30 and from 60. I use a different color chip for the numbers from 30 through 57 and a different color for the numbers from 60 through 87. Students who have very good visual memories will begin to use the visual pattern on the counting chart to help themselves say the numbers.

When the students are very fluent verbally on the threes up to 30 and are writing the pattern in speed drills, have them begin skip counting by fours at least up to 40. Have them put chips on the numbers on the counting chart at least up to 80 to see the repetitions in the pattern visually. They now have the skip counting chants for ones, twos, threes, fours, fives, and tens.

Using Skip Counting for Multiplying and Dividing

As soon as students understand that multiplying is just adding up same-size numbers, they can multiply by using these skip counting chants. To multiply 7×3 they can hold up seven fingers and count by threes as they put their fingers down or as they touch each finger. Second graders can do this quite easily if they have been taught to represent problems with semi-concrete materials (e.g., sticks or chips).

By the time they are doing this, they will know that 3×7 is the same as 7×3, so they can multiply any number from 1 through 10 by any number up through 5 (because they can skip count by 10, 2, 3, 4, and 5). Of course, skip counting isn't as fast as you want them to be, but it will allow them to compute products. The only products they will still need to compute by other means are:

6×6, 6×7, 6×8, 6×9, 7×7, 7×8, 7×9, 8×8, 8×9, and 9×9

There are several easy tricks for the nines that even very young children can learn (see the next section), so that leaves six facts; the doubles are easy for most students, which leaves four facts to learn by rote.

As they learn to multiply in this way, they can also be taught to divide by using their skip counting chants. They should understand the concept of division and be able to illustrate it in a variety of real-life problems before practicing these fact strategies.

To divide by 2, 3, 4, or 5, they are going to skip count until they reach the dividend (the total number they are going to divide up into groups). As they skip count they will put up a finger for each number they say. When they have reached the dividend, the number of fingers they have up is the answer to the problem.

For example, if a student wants to find out how many tickets each of the five members of his club will get if they divide 40 tickets up evenly, the student will count by fives until he reaches 40, putting up a finger for each number of the counting chant: 5, 10, 15, 20, 25, 30, 35, 40. He has eight fingers up and each member of his club will get eight tickets. Likewise, if he starts with 40 tickets and wants to know how many members can have tickets if he gives 5 to the members as they come in to the clubhouse, he will count by fives until he reaches 40. They can easily use the same strategy for computations with remainders (e.g., 42 tickets and five members means that each member will get eight tickets and there will be two left over).

This approach is very useful for estimating answers to problems, an important skill if students are going to use calculators to find specific answers to problems with large numbers. For example, here is a problem:

> The students have been collecting books for a sale to raise money for their trip to Washington DC. They have collected hundreds of books and the sale is this weekend so the books have to be put out on tables. To keep the books neat with the binding easy to read, the students have gotten a box company to donate boxes. They will cut each box in half

to make a tray and put the books in so that their bindings will be up. Donnal, Michael, Henri, and James are in charge of making up the boxes and cutting them in half to make trays. They want to know how many trays they need to make up. Karen, Leisha, Sonya, and Cassie are in charge of the paperbacks. They put paperbacks in five trays and count the number in each to get an idea of the number of trays they need. They find that an average of 23 paperbacks fit into each tray. They have about 850 paperbacks. How many trays do they need?

To estimate the answer, round 23 up to 25 and count by 25 until you get to the multiple closest to 85, which is 75. Three 25s are 75, so thirty 25s are 750. So 30 trays will get up to a little less than 750 books. There are a little more than 100 books left over, and counting by 25 to 100 is 4, so 35 or 36 trays should be about right. (The actual answer is 37 trays.)

Multiplying by Nines

Skip counting is just listing the successive multiples of a particular number. For the numbers 2, 3, 4, 5, and 10, the patterns are fairly clear and easy to learn directly. The multiples of 9 also follow a useful pattern, but one that may not be so easy to see. This section describes how to teach and use it.

The fastest computation device for nines is to hold up both hands, with fingers spread. Count from the left-most finger the number of nines you want and bend that finger down. Then the tens will be on the left of the folded down finger and the ones will be on the right. I find it easiest to have my palms facing me; the examples that follow are described from that viewpoint.

- For 9×3, bend down the third finger from the left, which is the middle finger of your left hand. The fingers to the left of that (your thumb and first finger) represent the tens, making *twenty*. The fingers to the right of your bent down finger represent the ones, making *seven*; $9 \times 3 = 27$.

- For 7×9, bend down the seventh finger from the left, which is the ring finger of your right hand. You now have six fingers to the left of that finger, making *sixty*. You have three fingers to the right of your bent down finger, making *three*; $7 \times 9 = 63$.

Many students have either figured out or been told the pattern of writing the numbers from 0 through 9 down a column and writing the numbers from 0 through 9 up a column to the right of the first set. The result will be the products of 1×9 through 10×9. The only difficulty with this is that most students do not connect the numbers in the answers with the correct questions. They have to write the entire sequence any time they want to multiply by 9.

The most useful computational device for students who are about 10 years old or older uses the fact that the digits in the multiples of nines through 10×9 add up to nine ($11 \times 9 = 99$, and from 12×9 through 20×9 the three digits in the answer add up to 9). Younger students can also learn this, but they have a hard time holding the steps in mind to get the answers. I taught it to my third graders and some of them could use it well, but others couldn't.

To teach this pattern, begin by listing the *nines* facts on the board, as in Display 10-2. The pattern is that the number of tens in the answer is one less than the multiplier of 9, and the digits in the answer have to add up to *nine*. I work on the pattern in two steps: the number of tens, and then adding the digits to get nine. One of the "extra" advantages of knowing that the tens and ones in the answer add up to *nine* is that it provides a very quick check on which number, 54 or 56 is the answer to 6×9 and which one is the answer to 7×8, answers that are very easily confused because they are so close together. The "nine problem" has to have an answer that adds up to *nine*.

$$1 \times 9 = 9$$
$$2 \times 9 = 18$$
$$3 \times 9 = 27$$
$$4 \times 9 = 36$$
$$5 \times 9 = 45$$
$$6 \times 9 = 54$$
$$7 \times 9 = 63$$
$$8 \times 9 = 72$$
$$9 \times 9 = 81$$
$$10 \times 9 = 90$$

Display 10-2

Step One: The Number of Tens in the Answer

Introduce the pattern by saying something like,

> There is an easy way to calculate *nine* times another number in your head if you can't remember the fact. We're going to work on that pattern today. Let's look at these facts. Point to 1×9. If we have *one nine*, we have what? (*"nine"*)

> Right. So we don't need to calculate for that. Let's look at 2×9. Point. *Two times nine* is *eighteen*. We have *two* here (point to the

2), and we have *one* ten here in *eighteen*. Point to 18. We went down from the *two* in the multiplier to *one* in the answer. Point again to the 2 and the 18.

If you haven't used the term "multiplier," substitute the term you have used, or stop and teach the term and then come back to this. It's not good to try to teach the term while doing this because many students won't be able to process all of the language fast enough to learn the mathematics.

If you have a student who wants to know why we go down from the multiplier, you can talk about the relationship between *two* times 10 being 20, and *nine* being one less than ten, so the answer for *two times nine* has one less *ten* in it. I find that some students see this more easily if you go through the pattern for all the nines first. If no one asks and no one seems to need more explanation to do the problems, don't bother teaching this idea explicitly until the students are very fluent at multiplying by *nine* and by *ten*. (Most of them will see it on their own.)

To continue teaching the nines pattern, say something like,

> *Three times nine* is *twenty-seven*. We have *three* here in *three times nine*. Point to the 3 in 3×9. And we have *two* tens here in *twenty-seven*. Point to 27. We went down from the *three* in the multiplier to *two* in the answer *twenty-seven*. Point again.

> *Four times nine* is *thirty-six*. We have *four* here in *four times nine*. Point to the 4 in 4×9. And we have *three* tens here in *thirty-six*. Point to 36. We went down from the *four* in the multiplier to *three* in the answer *thirty-six*. Point again.

> *Five times nine* is *forty-five*. We have *five* here in *five times nine*. Point to the 5 in 5×9. And we have *four* tens here in *forty-five*. Point to 45. We went down from the *five* in the multiplier to *four* in the answer *forty-five*. Point again.

> *Six times nine* is *fifty-four*. We have *six* here in *six times nine*. Point to the 6 in 6×9. And we have *five* tens here in *fifty-four*. Point to 54. We went down from the *six* in the multiplier to *five* in the answer *fifty-four*. Point again.

At this stage I cover up the answer to 7×9 and say, What will the first digit of the answer to *seven times nine* be? If the students can't respond immediately, I point to the previous facts one at a time while reminding them that we went down from *two* to *one* ten, from *three* to *two* tens, from *four* to *three* tens, etc. When I get to 7×9, I say, So we'll go down from *seven* to ? Virtually all the students will say *"six"*. If they don't say *"tens"*, I point to 63 and ask if they are tens or ones. I do the same with 8×9 and 9×9.

 Fast Oral Practice: Say something like, So that's the way we can tell what the tens in the answer is. We go down one from the number we are multiplying by. Let's practice that. I'll give you a fact and you tell me the number of tens in the answer. Do this fast oral practice on each fact in random order. If this is not quite automatic, or if you do not have time, introduce the next step in the next lesson. Practice this step each day for a few days until it is absolutely automatic.

Step Two: Adding the Digits to Get Nine

Introduce this step by saying something like,

Now you know how many tens are in the answer. Let's look at the answers to see what else you have to do. If we add the tens and the ones in these answers, what does each set add up to?

Run your finger down the answer column and point to each digit in the answers. Writing $1 + 8 = \underline{}$ beside 18 puts the question into an arithmetic statement. If necessary, write the addition statements beside each of the answers.

 Fast Oral Practice: Do this when it is clear to everyone that the digits in each answer add up to 9: Now I'll give you the tens in the answer and you tell me the answer. Remember that you have to add something to the tens to get nine. Here's the first one: *three tens.* (*"six"*) Do each of the facts, in random order. If your students do not add quickly and accurately, this will take considerable practice. You can put the two steps together before this step is automatic, but it's not an efficient strategy for multiplication until it is automatic.

Putting the Two Steps Together

Introduce this by saying something like,

Now we need to put these two steps together. I'll erase these answers and ask you to do both steps to get the answer to the fact. What is *six times nine*? Point. How many tens? (*"five"*) How many ones? (*"four"*) What's the answer? (*"fifty-four"*)

Do each fact this way, in random order. Practice each fact, in random order, for several days; it won't take more than a few minutes. Ask the students to verbalize the steps they use to get the answer. From then on, if they have a nines fact in a problem and don't answer automatically, ask them what they do to get the number of tens in the answer. Usually you do not have to ask for the next step, and you don't often have to prompt for the tens more than a couple of times.

If you want to continue past 10×9, begin with 11×9 and line up the statements vertically, as in Display 10-3, with a line below $11 \times 9 = 99$. Ask the students to look at the numbers for patterns. Often, students will mention that, starting with the ones in the last answer, you can just count up from *zero* to *nine*, and then you can count from *nine* to *eighteen* if you go down the tens. Confirm that they are right but that you wouldn't want to have to write out the whole list if you wanted to use just one of the products. After an appropriate wait time, if no one has mentioned that the digits in the answers from 108 through 180 add up to 9, encourage them to look at each answer and think about the answers of the previous set. Model your thinking if necessary: *one hundred eight* — if I add these digits, I get *nine*.

$$11 \times 9 = \ \ 99$$
$$12 \times 9 = 108$$
$$13 \times 9 = 117$$
$$14 \times 9 = 126$$
$$15 \times 9 = 135$$
$$16 \times 9 = 144$$
$$17 \times 9 = 153$$
$$18 \times 9 = 162$$
$$19 \times 9 = 171$$
$$10 \times 9 = 180$$

Display 10-3

That's all it should take for the students to see if the rest of them follow the same pattern. Ask the students to add the digits in each answer and write the 9 to the right of the problem. Then ask them to look at the multiplier and see what they have to do to decide how many tens are in an answer (two less than the multiplier). Go back to 11×9; if you have not worked on the numbers times *eleven*, you could write them out now and practice them.

If you want to continue the pattern, write the product statements and their answers right below the previous set. Talk about when the digits in the answer add up to *nine* and how many they need to drop back from the tens in the multiplier of nine. Draw a line after 20×9 and 22×9 and talk about the nines in the answers to those problems. Continue with the 30s or give the students a list of the statements and answers without lines added and have them find the patterns for homework.

Efficient Finger Addition

Although I expect my students to memorize the addition and subtraction facts, I also want them to use their fingers efficiently. This means that I want them to hold up the number of fingers representing the smaller addend in an addition problem, say the larger addend, and then count their fingers to get the sum. This will also help them calculate missing addend problems. I get the students automatic at several steps (explained below) before I ask them to do problems. Students should be automatic at counting up from any number before starting this activity.

One of the skills that should be automatic is putting up any number of fingers as a group. For instance, if I say *three* or show them 3, I want three fingers to come up together. I do not want students to have to put up one finger at a time while they count *one, two, three.* I don't care which fingers they put up, but if am working with young children who have not already developed a pattern I have them use their thumb as *one,* so *three* would typically be a thumb, index finger, and middle finger. Whichever fingers they use, it's best if they are consistent because this can become a visual memory device many of them will be able to see in their minds, so that they don't actually have to use their fingers.

Getting this skill automatic just takes practice. It is usually best to practice on two or three numbers at a time until these are automatic and then move to two or three more, reviewing the previous numbers regularly if the students are not using their fingers automatically while they work on arithmetic problems. Some students become automatic at this in four or five days; others take ten or more days. It is something you can practice while lining up for an activity change, and students are often willing to practice this at home when they see how efficient it is for adding. You can begin working on the next steps before this is completely mastered.

I work on the rest of the skills in response to written problems, using worksheets such as the one pictured in Display 11-1.

Practice Adding on Fingers

$$
\begin{array}{cccccccccc}
3 & 8 & 7 & 3 & 4 & 5 & 7 & 8 & 3 & 6 \\
+\,4 & +\,5 & +\,4 & +\,7 & +\,8 & +\,6 & +\,6 & +\,4 & +\,8 & +\,8
\end{array}
$$

$5 + 4 = \_$ $7 + 3 = \_$ $\_ = 8 + 3$ $5 + 6 = \_$ $\_ = 6 + 4$

$\_ = 4 + 3$ $\_ = 3 + 6$ $7 + 8 = \_$ $3 + 5 = \_$ $\_ = 7 + 5$

$$
\begin{array}{ccccccccccc}
5 & 6 & 7 & 4 & 5 & 4 & 5 & 8 & 4 & 3 & 6 \\
+\,7 & +\,3 & +\,4 & +\,7 & +\,3 & +\,6 & +\,8 & +\,6 & +\,7 & +\,8 & +\,3
\end{array}
$$

$4 + 5 = \_$ $6 + 4 = \_$ $\_ = 3 + 7$ $\_ = 3 + 4$ $8 + 4 = \_$

$6 + 7 = \_$ $\_ = 4 + 6$ $\_ = 8 + 3$ $5 + 7 = \_$ $3 + 6 = \_$

$$
\begin{array}{ccccccccccc}
7 & 3 & 7 & 8 & 4 & 4 & 5 & 6 & 5 & 4 & 7 \\
+\,5 & +\,5 & +\,3 & +\,5 & +\,3 & +\,5 & +\,3 & +\,5 & +\,8 & +\,8 & +\,3
\end{array}
$$

Display 11-1

The worksheet has problems containing only the numbers 3 through 8, for these reasons:

▷ For adding a number to *nine*, I teach students that the answer will be one less than the number plus 10. We then practice doing that fast with a list of facts in random order. Putting out flash cards with the problems on them works well. I work on subtracting *nine* from a *teen* number (e.g., 14 − 9) by teaching the students that the answer will be one more than the *teen* number minus 10. We practice this in the same way as for addition.

▷ I work on adding *one* and *two* by counting up from any number I say or show them, as described in Chapter 2.

▷ I don't teach children with language and/or memory problems to count backwards, but I do want them to be able to give me the number one lower than any number I say or show them, as described in Chapter 2. Developing a thorough understanding of and fluency with the counting chant almost always creates this fluency in saying one less than any number. Over the years, I have observed a couple of students who were unable to do this. (One was a fourth grader with IQ scores in the gifted range who had one of the most severe mathematics disabilities I have ever seen.) If you have a student who just can't seem to become automatic at this, add questions involving 2 to your activities and worksheets.

Using the worksheet, the students need to become automatic at identifying the smaller number in a problem and then putting up that number of fingers. I have students become automatic at identifying the smaller number first, so you can start this before students have finished the previous step of raising a set of fingers automatically. I do some oral work, having the students respond as a group. Model a few problems for them and then point to the problem and have the students tell you the smaller number. In addition to doing some oral work, have the students mark the smaller number in some way (e.g., circle, highlight, slash). If the students need more work on writing numbers correctly, they can trace the number. Timing them as a challenge will usually result in better progress.

When the students are automatic at saying and marking the smaller number and also at putting up all the fingers for a number at the same time, have them put up the number of fingers that represent the smaller number. If you are working with a group, you can point to a problem and have the students all hold up their hands so that you can check to see that they are accurate. This part of the sequence usually takes only a few minutes for two or three days.

Another skill that needs to become automatic is saying the larger number in the problems on the worksheet. Although it seems as though this shouldn't need separate work if the students can identify the smaller number, students who do not easily become automatic at language and/or arithmetic skills do need to practice this. It usually requires only a few days' practice, and takes only a couple of minutes each day. You can do just oral practice, just written practice, or a little of both.

When these three skills are automatic, it is time to put them together to answer problems. The students will hold up the number of fingers for the smaller number, will say the larger number, and then count up for each finger held up. At first, many students need to do something with each finger they count. This might be folding it down, touching it with their opposite hand, or even touching their nose with it. If they can't easily fold their fingers down as they count, encourage them to move as quickly as possible to just looking at each finger while they count. It's faster if they can do it accurately.

The only problem students sometimes have at this stage is wanting to count their first finger when they say the larger number. Usually all you need to do is explain that they have to count up for each finger and show them what will happen if they don't. I often have them do something physical as they say the larger number before they start counting up. For instance, I sometimes let them bang their fists (only once) on the table, and begin counting up after that. This is something that can be practiced during transition times and takes only a few problems for three or four days. I'll say a problem such as **seven plus four**, and the students will hold up four fingers, say *"seven"*, and count *"eight, nine, ten, eleven"* as they do something with the fingers they have held up. (Of course, if you have students who have already practiced this incorrectly, it will take longer.)

Once students have learned to add efficiently on their fingers, we practice missing addends, which is the same process they will use for subtraction. This time they will say the addend they are given and then count up until they are at the sum. The number of fingers up is the missing addend. Practice subtraction in the same way.

Sometimes people worry that students won't stop using their fingers for calculating if you let them get efficient at it. I have found that if you do speed drills on the facts, virtually all children will stop using their fingers for most calculations. They will often go back to their fingers if they are trying to do more than one thing at a time, as might often be the case in a real-life situation. It's important for them to have an efficient way to use their fingers. (How recently did you use a crutch of some kind when you were trying to calculate while doing something else like listening to a conversation? I often use my fingers for things like figuring out ages when I am teaching. I can't listen to my students or talk while trying to calculate.)

If I have a student who just won't give up counting on her fingers when I think she should, we gather some data. For a week we time and record how long it takes her to finish sets of problems I am sure she can do from memory, and I let her use her fingers. For the next week, we time and record how long it takes to finish the same sets of problems without using her fingers. Almost always, the second week is faster. Of course, the student has had more practice, but if she brings that up, I just say something like, **Of course. But that's why you don't need to use your fingers anymore.** If the speed doesn't seem to be any faster by about the third day of the second week, watch carefully to see what's happening. Sometimes the student is still using her fingers, just not obviously. Once in a while, students don't want to admit that they could go faster without their fingers. In that case, I just keep doing speed drills. Sometimes I have the students say the problem, and then I say the answer and have them write it down while saying it.

If you are working with students who have very severe arithmetic disabilities or severe memory problems, they may need to use their fingers or some other calculating strategy for almost every problem they do. As long as they understand the problems and how to solve them, that's fine.

 Teachers often ask me if I teach the so-called strategies or tricks for facts, such as $4+5 = 9$ because $5+5 = 10$ and 4 is one less than 5, or $6+7 = 13$ because $6 + 6 = 12$ and 7 is one more than 6, etc.

I do; but I am very, very careful to observe my students' ability to do this efficiently. Many students with processing and/or memory problems are not able to process the problem fast enough to decide which strategy, if any, to use and still have enough working memory left to remember what else the problem might be asking them to do. The processing task is easy for adding or subtracting consecutive numbers because you can always go up one or down one from a double. For multiplication, however, the student has to remember the fact for the square (e.g., 6×6) and then has to count up or down a long way to get the answer (e.g., up 6 for 7×6). This often results in errors, either in counting to get to the fact or in remembering what else a problem might be asking. These strategies or tricks often seem quite easy and efficient when students are calculating simple facts. However, when they are working on problems that require several steps, these strategies are not nearly as efficient as simply knowing the facts.

I have discussed this matter with Harry Sylvester, a successful mechanical engineer and past president of the Learning Disabilities Association of America who has severe dyslexia and associated language, memory, and processing problems. Harry is gifted in mathematics, but he had the same problems with arithmetic as are common to so many people with his disabilities. I asked him about learning the number facts. He said that it took a lot of time and effort to learn them, but then they stuck and he could use them. My experience with students mirrors Harry's experience. Of course, some of these students will "draw a blank" on a fact more often than the average student. For such times, it is useful to have strategies such as using the doubles, but if pressure has been the cause of the memory lapse, the processing required to use a strategy might be impaired, too.

Another question I get from teachers is, "Why not just let the kids use calculators, rather than their fingers?" My answer is, "I don't think that's a good idea." I'm not opposed to calculators; in fact, I approve of using them, especially for working with large numbers. However, young children who are slower at learning their facts are often also slow and/or inaccurate at using a calculator. Moreover, they often don't have the estimation skills required to tell them if the calculator's answer is even close to being correct. Almost all students have their fingers with them, available for use almost all the time. Getting out a calculator to do computations that can be done on your fingers or in your head has always seemed to me to be a waste of time and effort.

Linking Addition and Subtraction

The instructions in this chapter lead students to think of addition and subtraction as related operations, resulting in fluency in solving related addition, subtraction, and missing addend equations. *Speed Drills for Arithmetic Facts* (Oxton House, 2001) can be used to develop automaticity on these kinds of equations.

The prerequisite knowledge your students should have is listed below. If your students do not have all of this knowledge, you can teach it while you work through this material, using the extra problems listed in the Appendix. You will, however, have to add considerably to the instructions in order to teach the concepts and vocabulary. If you know that your students have some of this knowledge and can already do some of the tasks fluently, alter the instructions to add only what they don't know or can't do.

Prerequisite knowledge and skills:

1. Students must be able to name and write the numbers from 1 though 19 and to count this many objects. They must be able to read the number names (*one, two, three, . . .*). If they are able to do this up to 10 or 12, you can have them do the activities included in these materials as long as they are fluent at counting any values you will use for the activities. The materials for learning the counting chant (in Chapter 2) are useful for teaching the numbers above 10 to students who are not yet automatic at counting.

2. Students must be able to use a variety of ordinary, everyday words and sentences to describe problems and equations that represent the problems. They should be able to substitute arithmetic vocabulary and symbols for the everyday words and to use word cards to create these statements. (See the "materials needed" part below for notes on using word cards.)

For example, given an equation such as $4 + 6 = 10$, students should be able to provide problems such as, "Chandra has four pencils and Dixon has six pencils. How many do they have altogether?" They should be able to describe the equation by saying something like: *"Four and six is the same as ten"*, or *"Four and six make ten"*. They should be able to say, *"Four plus six equals ten"* and write $4 + 6 = 10$.

Students should be able to do the same with subtraction problems (e.g., *"Donny's cat had seven kittens. Donny has given four of them away. How many more does he have to give away?"*).

As you read through these instructions, if you find expressions that you know your students have not learned, either substitute appropriate expressions that your students already know or teach the expressions I use by using both sets of expressions interchangeably.

3. Students must know that whatever is on one side of an "=" sign has to be equal to whatever is on the other side of the "=" sign and be fluent at reading and writing arithmetic statements with the sum or difference on either side of the equal sign.

4. Students must know that addition is commutative and subtraction is not (but they don't need to use the word "commutative").

 Before going any further, let me explain one of my fundamental convictions about the skills students need to learn in order to become automatic at addition, subtraction, and missing addend problems. Many mathematics materials teach students to count backwards to subtract. **I never do that.** Although many students can count backwards with little trouble, many cannot. As most teachers have observed, the counting chant is not particularly easy for many students to master. Counting backwards is a different counting chant and is probably even harder to learn once the basic counting chant has been learned, because the same words are used in a different order.

There is absolutely no reason to count backwards for subtraction. The difference between any two numbers can be found easily by counting up from the lower number. Counting this way makes the relationship between addition, subtraction, and missing addend problems so clear that many students know where my questions will lead before I finish asking them. To me, practicing backwards counting is a waste of precious time. I do, however, want students to be able to tell me the number just before any number I give them.

Materials needed besides pencils and paper:

- Counters the students will use to represent problems (any uninteresting objects, such as bingo counters, stirring sticks, buttons, or pieces of construction paper). I refer to these things as "chips" in order to avoid confusion between "count" and "counters."

- Two pieces of yarn or string for each student, one about 30 inches long and one about 10 inches long.

    I like to use yarn or string to outline the area in which we will work on a problem. The shorter piece of yarn will divide the chips into sets when we work on subtraction. The chips not in use stay outside of this area. If you want to have the students represent quite large quantities with chips, use a longer piece to outline a larger area. The yarn can be overlapped for smaller areas. I usually tell students to make a circle with their string, but the shape doesn't matter, so if you have students who need to control part of the instruction, let them make any shape that is open enough to work in.

- Word cards for the numbers, the words you use to create arithmetic sentences, and the story facts for the problems you use.

    It is much easier to focus on the problems and keep students' attention if you use word cards than it is if you have to write out all of the problems. The easiest way to do this is to use magnetic strips and a magnetic white board or chalk board. If you don't have a magnetic board, you can make one with a piece of metal (e.g., a large cookie sheet) and white board material that has adhesive on one side.

    Examples of word cards you need, in addition to the number names, are: *is the same as, make, equals, and, take away, minus,* and/or any other words your students have been using for their arithmetic statements.

As you work through the problems, make cards for the story facts in the problems. (The following section describes how these cards are used.) Students need the same sets of word cards to describe problems you give them or problems they create.

- (optional) White boards for the students to write on.

    These are not essential, but they are very useful. The least expensive way of providing these is to go to a lumber supply store and get a sheet of shower board. You can cut it into any size pieces you want. I like to tape the edges because otherwise they are a bit rough and can peel or separate.

Creating the Addition Statements

Introduce the lesson and summarize what the students already know (background knowledge). Say something like:

> Today we're going to start working on the relationship of addition, subtraction, and missing addend statements. You already know how to write and solve problems that require addition and subtraction. The difference is that we will use one problem at a time to see which addition and subtraction statements match what we know about the problem.

> Here's a problem. The band is giving a concert and the students will all sit on the bleachers in the gym. Mrs. Gwynn, the principal, has invited some parents and tells Leah and Daniella to get chairs for the parents. Mrs. Gwynn tells Leah to get *three* chairs and Daniella to get *four* chairs. How many parents are coming? Show me with your chips.

If you have students who will not remember the problem, repeat that Leah was told to get *three* chairs and Daniella was told to get *four*. When the students have represented the chairs with their chips, ask how many parents are coming. If students put all their chips together right away, ask them to show you Leah's chairs separated from Daniella's chairs.

When they have all represented the problem, show them your story facts and practice reading them. (If you have been working on identifying the important facts in word problems *before* representing them with concrete materials, you might want to do that first, getting or writing out your story fact labels at that time.)

Put your story facts on the board and create the arithmetic statement in Display 12-1 as follows. Say something like,

> Good. Now let's use the story facts to create the arithmetic part of the problem on the board. Put out the story facts as you ask the questions.
>
> How many chairs did Leah get? (*"three"*)
>
> And how many did Daniella get? (*"four"*)
>
> So what shall I put here? Point to the spaces below the story facts. (*"three and four"*)
>
> Good. And what is *three and four* the same as? Put "is the same as" on the board. (*"seven"*)
>
> So how many parents are coming? (*"seven"*)

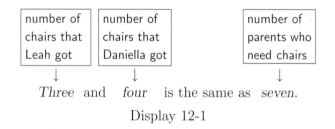

Display 12-1

Review the problem by saying something like,

> Let's review what the problem said and what it asked. Mrs. Gwynn invited some parents. Did we know how many were invited? (*"no"*)

If students say *"yes"*, go back to the original problem and ask them to show you the words that tell how many were invited. Reinforce that we didn't know, but we figured it out from the rest of the information in the problem.

> What did Mrs. Gwynn do that allowed us to figure out how many parents were coming?

The students should say something to the effect that she told Leah and Daniella how many chairs to get out and so we could add the chairs to tell how many parents were coming. You might have to ask what they did with the chairs that Leah and Daniella got out.

To work on the commutative property of addition, say something like,

> Let's look at other ways of writing the same thing. Will we get the same total if I put *"four* and *three"*? Put it next to the other sentence, as in Display 12-2, so that you don't have the numbers under the wrong girl. (*"yes"*)

> So we have *four and three* is the same as what? Put in "is the same as". (*"seven"*) Put that in.

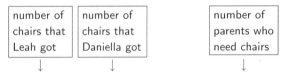

Three and   four   is the same as   seven.   Four and *three* is the same as *seven*.

Display 12-2

To work on writing the equation with the total on the left, put "is the same as" below the previous sentence and say something like,

> It doesn't matter if we have *three and four* or *four and three* (pointing to the sentences), we still get *seven*. Will we still get *seven* if I put *three and four* over here? Point to the right of "is the same as". (*"yes"*)

> Good, so I'll put that in. Put in *"four and three"*. And what is *four and three* the same as? (*"seven"*) So I'll put *seven* over here. Put it in. (See Display 12-3.)

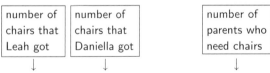

Three and   four   is the same as   seven.   Four and *three* is the same as *seven*.

Seven is the same as *four* and *three*.

Display 12-3

Now we've got *"Seven* is the same as *four and three."* What else can I say *seven* is the same as? Point while talking. (*"three and four"*)

If no one answers, point to the first two sentences, saying something like, Here we had *three and four* and here we had *four and three.* Down here I have *four and three.* What else can I have?

Next, substitute arithmetic symbols for the words in this problem. Put the numbers below the first example that has the word facts and put the other number statements to the right of the word statements.

Now we're going to substitute numbers and arithmetic symbols for the words. What should I put for this word? Point to the first number. And for this word? Point to the next word.

I do the numbers first and then go back to the + and = symbols, so that "3 + 4 = 7" is below the sentence at the left of Display 12-3. Substitute numbers for the words in all the sentences, ending up with what's above plus a third column, shown in Display 12-4.

$$4 \; + \; 3 \; = \; 7$$
$$7 \; = \; 4 \; + \; 3$$
$$7 \; = \; 3 \; + \; 4$$

Display 12-4

Have your students write these expressions in both horizontal and vertical form. They need to be able to read any of these statements, to create these statements when given a variety of word problems, and to create word problems when given a variety of these statements.

Creating the Subtraction Statements

Next I turn the problem into a subtraction problem, but I don't tell the students that because I want them to tell me what to do to solve the problem. Say something like,

Let's look at a different problem using the information about the parents who are coming to the concert. What if Daniella can't remember how many chairs she is supposed to get, but she knows that seven parents are coming, and Leah has already gotten her chairs out? What do we know and what can you show with your chips?

Most students will show the problem with no help. If you need to help, ask them to show you how many chairs they need for the parents and how many chairs Leah

got out. Have the students use the short piece of yarn to separate from the others
the chips representing the three chairs Leah has gotten. (They can move the chips
a little, too.)

Now write the problem out in words (or use word cards):

> **Let's write the problem out in words. How many chairs do they need
> for all the parents?** (*"seven"*) Put *seven* on the board.

> **How many chairs did Leah get?** (*"three"*) Put *three* a short way away
> from *seven*.

> Point to the space between the words and say, **What words should I put
> in here to show what we did?**

Students will usually suggest whatever words they have been taught (e.g., take
away, minus, less, etc.). If they suggest something that is clearly wrong, put it in a
separate place so that you can show later why it's not going to work. If they make
suggestions that include words specific to this problem, remind them that the words
have to be appropriate for any problem they can make up (e.g., you can't use names
of people because they'll change).

Finish the problem. Add "is the same as" and a line for the answer to the
sentence, and ask the students how many chairs Daniella got out. Put the word-fact
statements about the chairs above the numbers, as shown in Display 12-5. **Do not**
have the students count backwards from *seven* to get the answer. Have them count
the number of chips they have left after they separated the *three* for Leah's chairs.

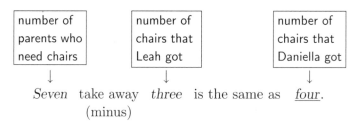

Display 12-5

Review the problem, saying something like,

> **We knew how many chairs we started with.** Point to *seven*. **We knew
> how many Leah got out.** Point to *three*. **We wanted to know how many
> Daniella got out. You put out** *seven* **chips for the chairs and moved**

three chips away for Leah's chairs. That left the *four* that Daniella got out.

Review the name *subtraction* by asking the students what they call this type of arithmetic statement. Then look at the opposite subtraction problem. Say something like,

> Now let's pretend that Leah forgot how many chairs she was supposed to get, so she waits for Daniella to get her chairs out. Show me with your chips what we know for this problem.

If your students don't quickly arrange their chips correctly, ask them how many parents are coming and have them show that. Then ask them how many chairs Daniella got out and have them separate *four* chips using the short piece of yarn.

> Let's write the problem out in words. Put the story facts and the words for the problem on the board as you ask the questions, as in Display 12-6.

> How many chairs do they need for all the parents? (*"seven"*)

> How many chairs did Daniella get? (*"four"*)

> What do we do to see how many chairs Leah has to get? (*"take away"*)

> Good. We knew we needed *seven* chairs altogether and Daniella got *four* chairs; so how many does Leah have to get? (*"three"*)

Again, **do not** have the students count backwards from *seven*. If they need to count, have them count the chips representing Leah's chairs.

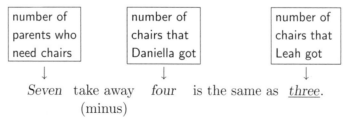

$$Seven \quad \text{take away} \quad four \quad \text{is the same as} \quad \underline{three}.$$
$$\text{(minus)}$$

Display 12-6

As with adding, also work on the statements when the answer is on the left side of the equation. Put "is the same as" below the previous sentence and ask the students if it matters which side of the equation the answer is on. Write each subtraction sentence with the answer on the left.

Add these four statements to your list of statements using numbers and the − and = symbols. If your students don't know both "take away" and "minus" as wording for subtraction, teach them these words, substituting either wording for the other and for whatever other wording they may be learning in their arithmetic program. In order for students to relate their school learning to their environment, they must learn the vocabulary they will hear in both environments. If you say the sentences using the variety of vocabulary they will hear, they will learn it. It always helps to point out the spelling patterns of the words, writing "minus" in separate syllables (*mi nus*) and saying it slowly while arcing under the syllables. Write the problems in vertical format, too.

If your students have not had previous practice using addition and subtraction for the same story problem, do three or four problems each day until they are automatic at moving their chips and creating the equations that go with the stories. They need to be able to tell you in the words of the story problem what the numbers and the chips represent for each equation. (Some additional problems appear in the Appendix.)

The next step is to add the missing addend problems. In any one lesson, do only as much of this as your students can attend to.

Creating the Missing Addend Statements

If you have had your students count up for subtraction problems (e.g., $7 - 3 =$ ___ means count up from 3 to 7), you have had them do missing addend problems. All you will be adding here is the notation. You can teach the students how to write missing addend statements from either addition or subtraction statements, but I prefer working from subtraction, so that is what is described in this section.

To introduce missing addends from subtraction, show the students how we can write the question in a different way. For the example of the chairs, say something like,

> We were working on finding out how many chairs one of the girls had to get, when we knew how many chairs we needed and we knew how many chairs the other girl already got. Let's say we know how many chairs Leah got and we want to find out how many Daniella needs to get. How did we write that?

You might get a variety of answers, which is good. List them and have the students tell how they are related. For example, students might say, *"total chairs take away Leah's chairs equals (is the same as) Daniella's chairs"* or *"seven take away three"*. Write out the sentences in numbers and put the story facts above them.

Next, put Display 12-7(a) on the board while saying something like,

> Now I want to ask the question in a different way. I want to start with the total number of chairs on one side of the equation, and I want to put Leah's chairs on the other side of the equal sign.

> Point out the inaccuracy of the statement by saying something like, But now the two sides of the equation aren't equal. *Seven* isn't equal to *three*. What's missing?

Again, the students might give you a variety of answers. Confirm that the chairs that Daniella got are missing and put that story fact card to the right of Leah's chairs while saying something like,

> You're right. I need to show where Daniella's chairs will be. We don't know how many she got, so I'll put a line under her chairs. (Now your display should look like Display 12-7(b) without the plus sign.)

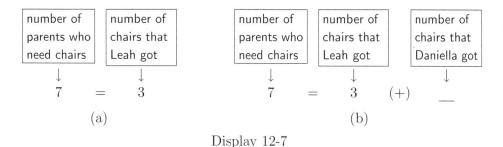

Display 12-7

Ask what sign they need to finish the statement:

> Now we know how many chairs Leah got. What do we have to do with Daniella's chairs to have both Leah's and Daniella's total *seven*? (*"add them"*)

> Good; so I put a plus sign here. Put it in. So now we know that Leah and Daniella got *seven* chairs altogether (point) and we know

that Leah got *three* of them (point) and we're going to add the chairs
that Daniella got. I'll read it with just the numbers: *Seven* equals *three*
plus what? How many chairs do I need to add? (*"four"*) Put in 4 on
the line.

Add the name "missing addend" to the problem by reviewing with the students
what we call the total in an addition problem (*sum*) and what we call each of the
numbers we add (*addends*). If you haven't used these labels in quite some time, just
remind the students what they are and ask them what was missing in this problem
(*an addend*). So we call these problems *missing addend problems.*

Using the story fact cards in the same positions, work on having Daniella's chairs
be the addend that is known and Leah's be the addend that is missing. Write the
new statement below the previous one (as in Display 12-8) and say something like,

> This time let's have Leah's chairs missing. We still know that together
> the girls got out *seven* chairs (point), and this time we know that
> Daniella got out *four*. Put 4 below Daniella's statement. So we have
> the addend for the chairs that Daniella got out, but the addend for
> the chairs Leah got out is missing. Put a line below Leah's statement.
> In numbers, we have *seven* equals something plus *four*. What goes in
> here? Point to the line. (*"three"*)
>
> Good. So the missing addend was *three*.

$$7 = 3 + \underline{}$$
$$7 = \underline{} + 4$$

Create all of the equations possible for the missing addend
problems. Say something like, Here are the missing addend prob-
lems we just created. Either read the problems as a group, or   Display 12-8
read them to the students. I use the wording, "*Seven* equals *three*
plus what?" ("*Seven* equals what plus *four*?") If your students need "is the same
as" instead of "equals," use those words. Then say something like,

> But we can write lots of missing addend statements with these numbers.
> What's another statement we can write?

If no one suggests one (e.g., $7 = 4 + \underline{}$ or $3 + \underline{} = 7$), suggest one or suggest
how they might think of one. For instance, Can we put the *seven* on the other
side of the equal sign? Generate all of these statements, listing them with the two
already written (the order doesn't matter), as in Display 12-9(a). Also write the
statements in vertical format, as in Display 12-9(b).

$$3 + \underline{} = 7 \qquad 4 + \underline{} = 7 \qquad 7 = \underline{} + 3$$

$$\underline{} + 3 = 7 \qquad \underline{} + 4 = 7 \qquad 7 = 4 + \underline{}$$

(a)

$$\begin{array}{cc} 3 & 4 \\ \underline{+} \quad \underline{+3} & \underline{+} \quad \underline{+4} \\ 7 \quad\; 7 & 7 \quad\; 7 \end{array}$$

(b)

Display 12-9

Go back and write the missing addends in on the lines, having the students read the problems as you fill them in, first saying "what" for the missing addend, then reading the problem with the number filled in. Review the name "missing addend" both by asking what part of the problem is missing and by asking what we call this type of arithmetic statement.

Review the names for all three statements you have been working on by putting examples on the board and asking the students what kind of statements they are. For example, say something like,

> Let's review the kind of arithmetic statements we've been working on. Here's one. Put $4 + 3 = \underline{}$ on the board. We have *four* plus *three* and we want to know what that equals. What do we call this type of statement? (*"adding, addition"*)
>
> Good. It's an addition statement. I'll put that out here.
>
> $$4 + 3 = \underline{} \qquad \text{addition}$$
>
> Here's another one. Put $7 - 4 = \underline{}$ on the board below the previous one and say, We have *seven* minus (take away) *four* equals. What do we call this type of statement? (*"subtraction"* or *"take away"*)
>
> Good. It's a subtraction statement. I'll put that out here:
>
> $$4 + 3 = \underline{} \qquad \text{addition}$$
> $$7 - 4 = \underline{} \qquad \text{subtraction}$$
>
> Here's another one. Put $3 + \underline{} = 7$ on the board below the previous one and say, We have *three* plus what equals *seven*. What do we call this type of statement? (*"missing addend"*) You might have to ask what's missing.
>
> Good. It's a missing addend statement. I'll put that out here:
>
> $$4 + 3 = \underline{} \qquad \text{addition}$$

$$7 - 4 = \underline{\quad} \qquad \text{subtraction}$$

$$3 + \underline{\quad} = 7 \qquad \text{missing addend}$$

Have the students write out all of the variations of these statements. I usually assign one group the addition statements, one group the subtraction statements, and another group the missing addend statements. We talk about an efficient way to divide up the task (e.g., horizontal versus vertical problems). I then time them so they do it quickly because it can take too long otherwise. An individual or small group can do it as homework or you can do one or two variations of each type of statement each day, adding to the previous statements until all of them are done.

Give the students a variety of problems to solve, or have them make them up themselves, and have them compare which type of statement each one wrote to solve the problem. If you do not get a variety of statements, assign different statement forms to different students. This is easily done by having the words "addition," "subtraction," and "missing addend" on separate cards and giving each student a card. Switching the cards around for each problem will give each student practice with the three different forms. You might also have to specify writing statements with the answer on a particular side of the equal sign and writing statements both horizontally and vertically. After doing a few of these problems, the students will get very fluent at thinking about how to write and solve problems.

At this point, students are now able to use any two numbers and their sum to form an addition statement, a subtraction statement, and a missing addend statement. This leads to fluency with number facts, especially if the students do speed drills that contain just three numbers, written in all the possible statement forms. The publication *Speed Drills for Arithmetic Facts* (Oxton House, 2001) contains speed drills set up in this way.

Linking Multiplication and Division

The activities in this chapter lead students to think of multiplication and division as related operations, resulting in fluency on multiplication and division facts and, later, on fractional parts of the products of these facts.

Prerequisite knowledge and skills:

1. Students should be fluent on the addition, subtraction, and missing addend concepts and activities of the previous chapter.

2. Students should be able to use a variety of ordinary, everyday words and sentences to describe situations and equations that represent multiplication problems. They should be able to identify the relevant numerical facts in the problems and to substitute arithmetic vocabulary and symbols for the everyday words.

   For example, given an equation such as $4 \times 6 = 24$, the students should be able to supply problems such as, *"We have four boxes of books with six books in each box. How many books do we have?"* They should be able to describe the equation by saying something like, *"Four times six is (equals) twenty-four"*, and write $4 \times 6 = 24$ (or $24 = 4 \times 6$).

3. The students should be able to do the same with division problems, and should be equally adept at finding the number of sets or the number of items in each set, depending on the wording of the problem.

   For example: Vinnie has twenty-four baseball cards and is going to give all of them to his friends. He has four friends. How many cards will each friend get? Will there be any left over? *or* Vinnie

103

is going to give his twenty-four baseball cards to his friends. He decides to give each friend six cards. How many friends will get cards?

4. The students should know that multiplication is commutative and division is not (but they don't need to use the word "commutative").

Materials needed besides pencils and paper:

- Counting chips of some kind, and squares (or other shapes) on which to put the sets or groups of counting chips.

    I have often cut and laminated squares out of two different colors of construction paper, so that we can compare the two different types of division problems. The lamination allows the students to label them with the appropriate story facts. For the last example above, the squares of one color would be labeled "friend 1," "friend 2," etc. (or they can be given names) and each square of the other color would be labeled "6 cards."

- Cards for the story facts for the problems you use and for the numbers and words you use to create arithmetic sentences (only if your students can't write them).

Creating the Division Statements

I start with a division problem because it seems easiest to change the problem from division to multiplication and then to a missing multiplier problem. I go through the problems much faster than I did with the addition and subtraction problems because, by now, the students should be very used to manipulating the story facts, the question, and the arithmetic statements.

Introduce the lesson and summarize what the students already know (background knowledge). Say something like,

Today we're going to start working on the relationship of multiplication, division, and missing multiplier statements. You already know how to write and solve multiplication and division problems. The difference is that we will use one problem at a time to see which division and multiplication statements match what we know about the problem.

Here's a problem: The state fair will start in a week. Jason and his three brothers have been saving money for several weeks and their grandmother has sent a check for $24.00 to be divided among them. How much will each boy get from their grandmother? Show me with your chips and squares what the problem will look like. The students should have four sets with six chips in each set.

Good. You have one set of chips for Jason and one for each of his brothers. They'll each get $6.00. Let's use a division sentence to represent that. What are the facts we are representing? (*"Jason and three brothers and the money"*) And what is the question we want to answer? (*"How much money does each boy get?"*) Put the fact and question cards on the board, as in Display 13-1.

Display 13-1

Good. What division statement do we need to represent this? (*"Twenty-four divided by four equals six."*) Put that on the board, as in Display 13-2.

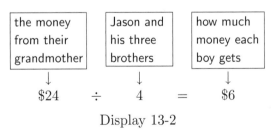

Display 13-2

Good. We have *twenty-four* dollars divided among the *four* boys, so each of them gets *six* dollars. Let's change the word cards to use language that could represent any problem. (If you haven't done much of this, just tell them what we can call the parts of the problem and review them a few times.)

What can we call the money from Grandmother? (*"the total"*) Replace the story fact card with "total," written or on a card.

What can we call Jason and his three brothers? (*"groups"* or *"sets"*) Replace the story card.

Good. Groups or sets. And what can we call how much money each boy gets? (*"the number in each group"*) Replace the story card.

Good. So we started with the total, the $24.00, and we knew how many groups we wanted to divide the total into, the four boys. We wanted to know how many would be in each group or set. And if we write the statement with a line for what we want to know, we'll have: $24 \div 4 = $ __. Write the statement below the words "total," "groups" (or "sets"), and "number in each group (or set)."

If the generic description of the parts is not an automatic part of your students' vocabulary yet, practice a few times by asking which of these (point to the three cards) is the total, which is the groups or sets, and which is the number in each group or set, asking in random order. Then have them name them as you point to them.

I don't often teach the formal language for each part of the problems (*dividend, divisor, quotient,* and *multiplicand, multiplier, product*). In fact, I would insist that the students use all of that vocabulary *only* if their school's math program uses it so extensively that the they won't be able to do the problems if they don't know the vocabulary. It doesn't help them understand how the problems apply to real-life situations, and it just adds more hard-to-remember vocabulary that is not used anywhere else.

However, it is convenient for communication if you use *product* and *quotient.* They are the results of multiplication and division, respectively, and are not particularly hard to learn. First, I tell the students what the words refer to, and work on their spelling and pronunciation. Write them in syllables (*pro duct, quo tient*), pronounce them while arcing under the syllables, spell them by syllables a couple of times. Do this daily until they become automatic. (You may have to tell them about the *ti* saying /sh/ if they haven't been introduce to words like *notion* and *vacation.* Then just say "total or product" when referring to multiplication, and "quotient or answer" when referring to division. If you are working with a story problem, you can ask for "the quotient, or number of sets" or for "the quotient, or the number in each set," as appropriate.

It seems to be hard for children to remember which number is the multiplier and which is the multiplicand, which is the divisor and which is the dividend. If you do teach this vocabulary, use the meaning of the suffixes *-er* and *-or* to help the students figure out which word is which. These suffixes mean "someone or something that does something." Think of the *divisor* as the number that does something: it divides the dividend into parts. (The quotient is the number of parts.) The *multiplier* multiplies (adds up copies of) the multiplicand to get the product. For several days you will probably have to ask what the suffix means and how that will help them remember which word is which.

To change the problem into a situation where the amount (of money) in each set or group is known but the number of sets (in this case, people getting money) is not known, you can say something like,

> Now let's look at what we would show if Grandmother had sent the $24 check with instructions to give **everyone** six dollars. If she didn't tell them who "everyone" was, what would the question be? (*"How many people will get money?"*) If the students have trouble with this, ask how many people would be in the family if you count one or two parents.
>
> Use your chips and squares to show me how they can figure out how many people will get money. Use the fact and question cards and write your arithmetic statement to show what you did.

The students can work in groups of two or three. They should end up with something that looks like Display 13-3.

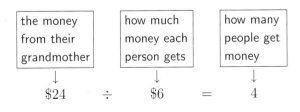

Display 13-3

So we have *twenty-four* dollars from Grandmother divided into sets of *six* dollars each. That means *four* people will get money. For whom do you suppose Grandmother intended the money? (*"the boys"*)

So this time we knew the total (point to $24), and we knew how much would be in each set (point to $6), and we wanted to know how many sets we would have. You wrote it like this. $24 ÷ $6 = ___ Write it below the word cards.

Review the two division problems by saying what we know and what we want to find out in each of them while pointing to the numbers and the lines.

Let's think of how else we can write these. Write the two equations on the board.

Do we have to have the line for the answer last, or can we have it to the other side of the equal sign? (*"It can be on either side"*)

Good. So tell me how else I can write these. Write "___ = $24 ÷ 4 or ___ = $24 ÷ 6" below the other statements on the right.

I'll write the other division statements and we'll go through what they say.

Write the following statements and review what each statement tells you (total, number of sets, or how many in each set) or asks you to find:

$24 ÷ ___ = $6 $6 = $24 ÷ ___ $24 ÷ ___ = 4   4 = $24 ÷ ___

Creating the Multiplication Statements

Now let's pretend that Jerrod, one of Jason's brothers, forgot how much money Grandmother sent, but he knows they each got six dollars. Use your chips and circles to show me how he can figure out how much money Grandmother sent. Use the fact and question cards and write your arithmetic statement to show what you did.

The students can work in groups of two or three. They should end up with some form of Display 13-4. (The multipliers can be in either order and the answer can be first.)

If your students have the word cards and numbers in different orders, have them compare results to confirm that it doesn't matter if the answer is first or if the multipliers are switched. Be sure that they can use the story facts in the statements, using "what" for the

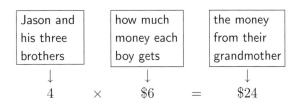

Display 13-4

missing fact (e.g., what is equal to the money each boy gets times the number of boys). If everyone put them in the same order, have them all write the number statements in all the variations possible:

$$4 \times \$6 = \$24 \qquad \$6 \times 4 = \$24 \qquad \$24 = 4 \times \$6 \qquad \$24 = \$6 \times 4$$

Go back through each statement, substituting the generic arithmetic vocabulary for each fact and question (the total, the number of sets or groups, and the number in each set or group).

> Now let's pretend that Jason put his money with the money he had saved. When he went to the fair, he couldn't remember how much of his money was from Grandmother. He could remember that Grandmother sent twenty-four dollars and each boy got the same amount. Show me with your chips and word cards how Jason can figure out how much of his money is from Grandmother.

> Write the problem with a line for the answer spot. There are several different ways to think of the problem. See how many you can write. Move your word cards around if you need them to help you think of the different ways to write the problem.

One of their statements should look like Display 13-5. They should also have:

$$\_\_ \times 4 = \$24$$

$$\$24 = \_\_ \times 4$$

$$\$24 = 4 \times \_\_$$

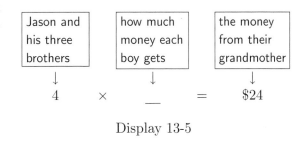

Display 13-5

Again, go back through each statement, substituting the generic arithmetic vocabulary for each fact and question (the total, the number of sets or groups, and the number in each set or group).

Give the students another problem and have them write out all the division and multiplication statements they can create for the problem. Be sure that they can also use the story facts and frame the question for each statement. If you have them work in small groups, with each group assigned a set of statements, it won't take too long for them to generate all the statements. Here is another sample problem:

> The librarians are cleaning out the young children's section of the library. They have 48 books that they want to get rid of. They decide to put the books into bags and give the bags to families. They put *four* books in each bag. How many families will get bags of books?

Do one or two problems each day until all of your students are very fluent at creating all possible forms of the multiplication and division statements. They can also make up problems themselves, and/or you can give them the multiplication and division statements and some story facts and have them create the questions that go with each statement.

Add some problems that have remainders. I give them cards with the word "remainder" on them so they can put the number left over under that card. (Write the word on the board with spaces between the syllables and talk about how it is spelled: *re main der*.) I add the notation "*R*" when they are fluent at using the word while working on their problems and in their oral language when they describe the problem. If they are writing their descriptions, the word also needs to be spelled correctly before they can switch to the *R*.

When the students are fluent at thinking about these related problems, work on memorizing the facts. The speed drills are effective, efficient ways to get these memorized. (See *Speed Drills for Arithmetic Facts*, Oxton House, 2001.)

In addition to the speed drills, there are a few visual displays that often help students learn and recall the multiplication and division facts. Each has advantages for a related mathematical skill. When I was using Cuisenaire rods for teaching mathematics to primary grade students, I created a visual display that has proven to be very useful over the years. I had become very frustrated with the traditional multiplication chart that was in our basal series and is included in almost all elementary mathematics materials. (See Display 13-6.)

The biggest problem with this chart is that the students who have trouble with memorizing their facts often have trouble using the chart. By the time they have followed the column and row for the numbers they are multiplying, they have often forgotten the numbers! Many times they can't follow both the column and row accurately. Moreover, this

×	1	2	3	4	5	6	7	8	9
1	1	2	3	4	5	6	7	8	9
2	2	4	6	8	10	12	14	16	18
3	3	6	9	12	15	18	21	24	27
4	4	8	12	16	20	24	28	32	36
5	5	10	15	20	25	30	35	40	45
6	6	12	18	24	30	36	42	48	54
7	7	14	21	28	35	42	49	56	63
8	8	16	24	32	40	48	56	64	72
9	9	18	27	36	45	54	63	72	81

Display 13-6

chart doesn't make the factors of the numbers clear, nor does it show visually how quickly the size of the products grows in relation to the numbers being multiplied.

Using the multiplication "trains" of the Cuisenaire rods, I made a chart that illustrates these relationships. The first one matched the lengths of the rods, which are in centimeters, so it was small. I then made a large one to put on the wall in my third grade class. When I began teaching at the college level and supervising clinical and practicum courses, I went back to using the smaller chart that I can carry with me easily. A foldout sheet at the end of this book is a copy of that chart without the colors described below. You can copy and color it or you can make your own; using a color printer makes it easy to produce multiple copies fast.

The diagonal row of numbers on the left are multiples of *one* and have parentheses around them, which becomes important when we work on factors of numbers. Of course, in the mid-sixties, I made everything by hand. That meant that I could easily write the numbers in the rows in colors that matched the Cuisenaire rods. The row of *twos* was red, the *threes* were green, the *fours* were purple, the *fives* were yellow, the *sixes* were dark green, the *sevens* were black, the *eights* were brown, the *nines* were blue, and the *tens* were orange. That made it even easier to follow across the rows. I recommend using some colors if you use the chart, just because the rows are so long to look across. The colors of the Cuisenaire rods are designed to make relationships apparent: 2 and 4 are red and purple, and 8 is brown; 3 and 6 are green and dark green, and 9 is blue; 5 and 10 are yellow and orange. It doesn't hurt to use such relationships.

We used the chart to practice skip counting. Then, to multiply, the students just counted by the multiplier as many times as the multiplicand specified. So 4×6

is *four* of the *sixes*; in the *six* row, go over four numbers and the product is the top number, 24. To divide, find the quotient at the top (the product of the multiplication problem), go down to the dividend on the left and count how many numbers there are up to the quotient; 27 divided by 3 tells you to start at 27, go down to the *three* row and count how many numbers there are up to 27.

One of the most useful relationships that this chart makes apparent for elementary school children is the relative size of the products when you multiply. This helps with estimation. In fact, I am convinced that one reason it seems easier for lots of children to learn multiplication facts than it is to learn addition facts is that the products are very spread out. It is much harder to remember distinctions between numbers that are close together than between those that are far apart.

As soon as the students have looked at the relationships between multiplication and division problems, they can use this knowledge for the division facts for products up to 100. The rows are numbered from 1 and 10 (on the left). If we think of a number in the first row as a product, then the other rows in which that number appears identify pairs of factors of that product, as follows: The smallest and largest of those factors go together as multipliers and, if there are four numbers, the two middle factors go together. For example, 30 appears in rows 3, 5, 6, and 10, so 30 is 3×10 and also 5×6. If one or three numbers appear below the top number, one of them is a double factor (the square root of the top number). For instance, 36 is 4×9 and also 6×6. (Not all of the factors up to 10 are accounted for in this way; the dots, as described below, identify the others.) With younger children you may not want to use the term "factors," but they can certainly see the patterns. When they do encounter the word, it will make perfect sense to them.

Some of my third graders who saw patterns very well made important observations about the chart. I did not continue the multiples of numbers past 10 times the number. I did that on purpose, so that they could see the patterns more easily, without the clutter that filling in the whole chart with every multiple of a number would produce. (To see what it would look like, on a chart that you won't use, fill in all the *twos*, all the *threes*, all the *fours*, etc., all the way to 100.) As a pattern, we worked on the multiples of *two* being even numbers and all even numbers being divisible by *two* (having *two* as a factor). So we didn't need to put the *twos* in. As I let them work with the chart and look for patterns, several of them observed that if you looked at the row of a number that was a double of a smaller number (e.g., 6 and 3), you could fill in the smaller number between each of the larger numbers. To keep the chart "clean," we decided that adding dots would be good. So, in the row of *sixes*, we added light green dots where all the other *threes* would go (below 9, 15, 21, 27, 33, 39, 45, 51, and 57).

When we began to work more on factors, they wanted to fill the whole chart in, using dots of the appropriate colors. At this stage, it was better to start with a new chart and keep the factors in their correct rows (the *threes* stayed in that row rather than being added to the *sixes* row). We put in the *twos* to see the factor patterns. I had them look for patterns such as which numbers had the most factors and which numbers had the least. I had them look at the odd numbers that had factors and had them describe the factors. If a number had only one factor on the chart, they divided the number by the factor to see what the pair was (e.g., 87 has factors of 3 and 29). They then looked to see if the pair (e.g., 29) had any other factors. I asked them to predict what they would find if they took a number that didn't have any factors (e.g., 13) and multiplied it by two. This got a bit complicated for third graders, but they made charts of numbers as they figured. They were able to describe quite a few patterns. All of this helps develop fluency in thinking about the number system. In a remedial setting, I would weigh the time it takes for some of this against what I know I must cover during the time I have the students. This kind of activity often is good homework.

Some years ago, a student[1] in one of my classes at Southern Connecticut State University showed me the visual device in Display 13-7. It consists of triangles that have the product (the dividend) at the top of the triangle and the multiplicand and multiplier (the divisor and the quotient) at the bottom. These diagrams illustrate the multiplication and division facts and lead into fractional parts of whole numbers very nicely. As I have described them to many teachers, they have put each set of facts (e.g., the *threes*) on a long chart that they put up on a wall until the students are absolutely automatic at using them. Several groups of these appear in a foldout chart at the end of this book. You can enlarge them on a photocopier if you want to use them with a group or post them on a wall.

Display 13-7

[1] Sarah Eighmy of New Haven, Connecticut.

Fractional Parts of Whole Numbers

When students have learned the concept of dividing items into sets of equal sizes, it is easy to switch to using fraction notation and to work on the fractional parts of the division (and multiplication) facts they have been using. For example:

> If 24 items have been divided equally into 8 sets, there are 3 in each set. Therefore, one of the *eight* parts is *three*. If *one* of the *eight* parts is *three*, then *two* of the *eight* parts is *six*, *three* of the *eight* parts is *nine*, and so forth.

> If the 24 items have been divided in *three* equal parts, then there are *eight* in each part, so *one* of the *three* parts is *eight*, *two* of the *three* parts is *sixteen*, and *three* of the *three* parts is 24.

If the students cannot say, read, and write the word "fraction," write it on the board in syllables (*frac tion*), pronounce it a few times while arcing under the syllables, have them read it with you, spell it aloud, and write it. If they don't know the spelling *-tion* for /shun/, it's a good time to talk about it. One of the few real rules in English spelling is that we don't use *-shun* to spell /shun/ at the end of multisyllable words. We use *-tion* far more often than any other spelling, so if you hear /shun/ at the end of words like *fraction*, *nation*, *vacation*, *motion*, and *action*, and you don't know for sure that it's spelled some other way, use *-tion*. You will probably be right.

Working on the Concept

Materials needed besides pencils and paper:

- their counting chips, and

- their squares (or other shapes) to put equal sized sets on.

To introduce this to students, say something like,

> Today we're going to use what you have been learning about division to create fractions. I'd like you to show me this problem with your counting chips:
>
> > Mr. Felton's third grade is going to raise money by selling plants. Mr. Felton has several different kinds of seeds and the students are going to choose which seeds they want to plant. Any seeds left over will go into the school garden. Three students choose to raise beans. The package has 24 beans in it. How many beans will each student plant?

When the students have divided up the bean seeds, they should have *eight* in each set. Have them write the division expression on their papers and write it on the board: $24 \div 3 = 8$.

To introduce the written notation for the fraction, say something like the following, writing the appropriate symbols as you say it:

> We can think about a division problem as a fraction. If we want to change the way we write this problem, we can just put a line in for the division sign. We can either use a diagonal line like this:

$$24/3 = 8$$

> or we can write the 24 above the 3 with a line between them, like this:

$$\frac{24}{3} = 8$$

> But there's a better way to describe it and write it because we can do more things with it. This is the way we describe it. Write out the words as you say them.

> > "One of the three equal parts of twenty-four is eight."

> Now let's put arithmetic symbols in for the words. I'll put the numbers and equal sign in first and then we'll read it together.

Write it again right below the previous sentence with the numbers and then read it in the same way:

"One of the three equal parts of twenty-four is eight."

" 1 of the   3 equal parts of   24   =   8 ."

Now I'll put the fraction in. We use the line to represent the words "of the" and the fraction tells us that we mean equal parts. So it will look like this:

$$\frac{1}{3} \text{ of } 24 = 8$$

We'll read this together. Remember that the line means "of the," and we'll say "equal parts" after saying the *three*. Let's go. (*"One of the three equal parts of twenty-four equals eight."*)

Good. Move one of the three equal parts of twenty-four you got with your counting chips to the side of your desk.

You can have them put a string around one of the sets instead of moving it if you think that seeing the sets in closer proximity would be better. If students are working in a group at a table, having them move the piece of paper on which they have the set might result in more movement or space than is useful.

Now move another equal set over to that same side. Now how many equal parts of twenty-four do you have over to the side? (*"two"*)

Good, you had *one* and now you have *two*. How shall I change this equation to show that we are talking about *two* equal parts instead of *one*? (*"Put a 2 in place of the 1."*)   Write "$\frac{2}{3}$ of 24" just below the previous equation.

What else do I have to do? If I change this side of the equation (point), what do I have to do to this side?

You will probably get *"change the eight to sixteen"*, which is correct. I want to show them that it's *two* sets of *eight* and it's always nice if a student volunteers that. If no one does, ask them how they got the *sixteen* and tell them that's what you'll write in first. Write it in as 2 *eights* so that you have $\frac{2}{3}$ of 24 is 2 *eights*. Have them read the equation with you and then write $\frac{2}{3}$ of 24 = 16 right below it.

Do *three* of the *three* equal parts the same way. Then add the word "thirds." By the time you are working on this, your students should have been introduced to the fraction words, but I've often found that students who are having problems in mathematics haven't learned all of the vocabulary that has been introduced. It often depends on what they have heard and used at home. I ask,

> **Do you know how we describe this** (point to $\frac{1}{3}$) **instead of saying "one of the three equal parts"?**

If no one volunteers *"one third"*, I say something like,

> **How about *one third*?** I point to the 1 and the 3 as I say it. **We use *third* for *three*. Have you used that before?**

Most students will confirm that they have, but it doesn't really matter. I just want them to think back to something they probably know and just didn't recall. If they can tell the ordinal position of items (*first, second, third, fourth,* etc.), refer them to that vocabulary.

> **If this is *one third*, what would this be?** Point to $\frac{2}{3}$.

If they don't say *"two thirds"* easily, point to the fractions and say,

> **If *one* of the *three* equal parts is *one third*, then *two* of the *three* equal parts is *two thirds*. Say that.** (*"two thirds"*)
>
> Point to $\frac{3}{3}$ and ask, **And how would we say this?** (*"three thirds"*)

If they have needed help with these labels, review them by asking them to label each one about three times. Point to them randomly, helping with the labels only if you need to.

If this has been easy for your students, you might want to show the students the form 1/3, using a diagonal line, so that when they start using fractions in their descriptive writing they can use whichever is convenient.

Leave the previous problems in view and switch the problem around:

> **Leave that problem on your desk and show me this problem:**
>
> > **Mr. Felton has 24 squash seeds and *eight* students want to plant squash seeds. How many seeds does each student get?**

Have them put out eight circles or squares and put their counting chips on each one. Have them write the division statement and put it on the board $24 \div 8 = 3$.

Now how many equal parts do we have? (*"eight"*)

Good. Move (or, put your string around) one of the *eight* equal parts.

Keep saying "equal parts" so that this becomes part of their thought process. **How shall I write that?** They may describe the fraction statement right away, but write the equation out in words first, using numerals but no other mathematical symbols. Then write it in fractional notation:

$$1 \text{ of the } 8 \text{ equal parts of } 24 \text{ is } 3.$$

$$\tfrac{1}{8} \text{ of } 24 = 3$$

Let's read this together. (*"One of the eight equal parts of twenty-four is (equals) three."*) So *one eighth* of *twenty-four* is *three*.

Now move another set of *three*. (Or, Put your string around *two* of the sets of *three*.) This time you write the statement. Write it like this one, showing the fraction. Point to the second statement, above.

Continue writing out the statements for *three* sets of *three*, and then for *four* the sets of *three*, and so on. Be sure to include all eight sets among the statements you work on. Write them in a column and leave them on the board so that you can discuss what happened on each side of the equal sign. Pointing to the appropriate problems, say something like,

Let's look back at these problems and review what happens on each side of the equal sign. Here we show that one of the *eight* equal parts of *twenty-four* is *three*. So *one eighth* is *three*.

Here we show that *two* of the *eight* equal parts of *twenty-four* is *six*. How many *threes* is *six*? (*"two"*)

Good. So *two eighths* is *two* of the *threes*, or *six*.

Continue with the rest of the examples, filling in the appropriate numbers in the following sentences.

Here we show that ___ of the *eight* equal parts of *twenty-four* is ___. How many *threes* is ___? (*"___"*)

Good. So ___ *eighths* is _____ of the *threes*, or ___.

I usually do at least one more day of problems like this and then I introduce using the triangles as an organizer for calculating. Examples from school situations might be such things as helping the physical education teacher mark the new basketballs or helping the librarian sort books and magazines. A problem from outside the school might be something like helping to sort materials for a building project.

Introducing the Triangles

If you have been using the triangles as a visual reminder of the relationship between multiplying and dividing, you can now work on using them to calculate the fractional parts of the whole numbers. I like to use one of the problems we have just worked through to introduce this. For example, I would put out the set of triangles for the threes (the numbers on the top are the multiples of three), and say something like,

> Today we're going to work on using our multiplication and division triangles to calculate fractions. Let's use the problem of the third grade class planting seeds to see how we can use the triangles. *Three* students wanted to plant beans and there were 24 bean seeds. How did you find out how many bean seeds each student got? (*"divided 24 into three equal parts"* or *"took one-third of 24"*)
>
> Good. We started with 24, so let's look at the triangle that has 24 at the top. Point as you review the division problem, and then write the arithmetic statement.
>
> *Twenty-four* divided by *three* is *eight*. How do we write it as a fraction? (*"One third of twenty-four equals eight."*)

They might tell you where to put the numbers and lines. That's fine, just read it when you have finished writing it. Point to the 3 on the triangle and say something like,

> So *one* of these *three* equal parts is *eight*; one student will get *eight* seeds. When we wanted to know how many seeds *two* students got, what fraction did we write? (*"two thirds"*)
>
> Right; we wrote two thirds of 24 (write it as you speak), and how much was that?

You want to get both *"two eights"* and *"sixteen"* as responses. If the students just say *"sixteen"*, ask them how many *eights* that is. When you get *"two eights"*, point to the 3 and say,

> Good. We have *two* of these *thirds*, so we need *two* of these *eights*. Point to the 8. And how much is *two eights*? (*"sixteen"*)

> Good. So if we want to know what *one third* of *twenty-four* is, we go to the *twenty-four* triangle (point), and we want *one* of the *thirds* (point), and that's *one* of these *eights*.

> If we want *two* of these *thirds* (point), we want *two* of the *eights* and that's *sixteen*.

> If we want *three* of the *thirds*, how many of these *eights* do we want? (*"three"*)

> Good; and what's *three eights*? (*"twenty-four"*) Good.

> Now let's look at the problem of *eight* students wanting to plant *twenty-four* squash seeds. How can we write that as a division problem? Point as you review the division problem and then write the arithmetic statement.

> *Twenty-four* divided by *eight* is *three*. How do we write it as a fraction? (*"One eighth of twenty-four equals three."*)

Again, they might tell you where to put the numbers and lines. That's fine; just read it when you have finished writing it. Point to the 8 on the triangle and say something like,

> So *one* of these *eight* equal parts is *three*; *one* student will get *three* seeds. When we wanted to know how many seeds *two* students got, what fraction did we write? (*"two eighths"*)

> Right, we wrote *two eighths* of 24 (write it as you speak), and how much was that?

You want to get both *"two threes"* and *"six"* as responses. If the students say *"two threes"*, point to the 8 and say,

> Good. We have *two* of the *eighths*, so we need *two* of these *threes*. Point to the 3. And how much is *two threes*? (*"six"*)

Good. So if we want to know what *one eighth* of *twenty-four* is, we go to the *twenty-four* triangle (point) and we want one of the *eighths* (point), and that's one of these *threes*.

If we want *two* of these *eighths* (point), we want *two* of these *threes*, and that's *six*.

If we want three of the *eighths*, how many of these *threes* do we want? (*"three"*) Good; and what's *three threes*? (*"nine"*)

Good. So what do we say if we want to know how many seeds *three* students will have? (*"three eighths"*) Good; we want *three eighths* (point), so how many *threes* (point) do we need? (*"three"*)

Let's review. If you start with *twenty-four* and divide it into *eight* equal parts (point to 8), one part will be *three*. Point to 3.

Point to the appropriate numbers while continuing with, If we want to know how many *two* of these *eight* equal parts is, we need *two* of these *threes*. If we want to know how many *three* of these *eight* equal parts is, we need *three* of these *threes*.

If I want to know how many *five* of these *eight* equal parts is, what do I need? (*"five of the threes"*)

Continue with as many more as you need to get your students very fluent at answering.

 Fast Oral Practice: The next step is to switch to using fractional parts of the whole number and do some fast oral practice. Start this when your students are fluent at the previous task and when you have time, reviewing the previous task if you start this on another day.

Practicing the Standard Language for Fractions

Display one of the triangles and shift to the standard terminology by saying,

Now I'm going to ask you to tell me the answers to the same questions, but I'm going to ask you the questions as fractions. If I say something like, "I want *one eighth* of *twenty-four*" (point to the 8), I want you to say "one three" (point to the 3) or "one of the threes." Here are some problems.

Dictate the questions for *one eighth* through *eight eighths* in random order. Do the same with *thirds* of *twenty-four*. Do at least one more set of problems from one of the triangles. Then have the students practice the wording of the problems by having them give the question (*"one-eighth of twenty-four"*, *"two thirds of twenty-four"*, etc.). They can work in pairs, but you might want to work with any students who have real difficulty with oral language statements. Again, let them get fluent at this before going to the next step.

The final step is to put the wording of the problem together with the answer multiplied out. I'll say something like,

> Now when I ask you the problem, you are going to tell me the answer in one number.
>
> For example, if I say, "What's *three eighths* of *twenty-four?*" you will say *"nine"*, instead of *"three threes"*, because *three threes* equals *nine*. All that's changing is that you are going to do the multiplication before you answer.
>
> Look at the triangle if it helps you do the calculation.

Take plenty of time working through a couple of problems, asking the students to think of __ of the *threes* if they need that step in order to process the problem and retrieve the answer. Again, practice with different whole numbers until the students are fluent.

These last sets of practice have been oral and just with numbers. Have the students work from written problems. Also give them some real-life problems and have them choose the triangle to use (the number of things that are being divided up). Sometimes we focus so much on the calculation part that we forget that **the first step is to be sure the students have figured out the facts from the word problem and can begin at the right place.** Time invested in making sure that students understand and can do this first step well will pay handsome dividends in all their future math work.

Appendix

Extra Problems

These problems have somewhat complicated stories, but they are typical of the messiness of the real world. Drawing pictures to represent situations helps students comprehend the problems. This will help students figure out what is relevant to the question they are trying to answer and what is irrelevant.

The sequence of the problems is not important, but if there are several parts to a problem, they should be given to the students one at a time. If students are working independently on the problems, either as individuals or in groups, just cut the problems into strips and be sure that they have completed one part correctly before giving them the next part.

For Addition and Subtraction

Problem A: It's Pat's birthday and her mom is making a cake.

1. Pat wants green candles. Her mom has four and tells Pat's brother, Sam, to get five more at the store on his way to his game. How old is Pat?

   Write all the statements that show how you can figure this out.

2. Sam forgot how many candle he was supposed to get but he knows it's Pat's ninth birthday and they have four candles. How can he figure out how many candles to get?

   Write all the statements that will show how he could figure this out. Write both addition and subtraction statements.

Problem B: Isaiah and Justine are planning their Halloween party.

1. Their mother needs to know how many gift bags she'll get for the party favors. Isaiah wants to invite six friends and Justine wants to invite five friends. How many bags will she need for all of the children? Don't forget Isaiah and Justine.

   Write all the statements that show how you can figure this out.

2. Isaiah likes to make up new board games. He is planning one to play with his friends at the party. He needs to make the boards but can't remember how many friends he invited. He finds the gift bags Mom bought and knows Justine is inviting five friends. How can he figure out how many boards he'll need for himself and his friends?

   Write all the statements that show how he can figure this out. Write both addition and subtraction statements.

3. Justine has watched Isaiah make his game boards. She thinks about what she can do that would be special for herself and her friends. Her favorite color is yellow so she decides to make yellow place mats for the table she will sit at with her friends. But she forgot how many friends she invited. If she knows how many gift bags her mother bought and how many game boards Isaiah has made, how can she figure out how many place mats she needs to make?

   Write all the statements that show how she can figure this out. Write both addition and subtraction statements.

Problem C: The Carsons raise Newfoundland dogs. Several mother dogs have had puppies, so the Carsons have lots of puppies and they are getting to be the age to sell.

1. A pet store in New York wants four puppies. A pet store in Montana wants seven puppies and the owner has picked the ones from one litter that she wants. The puppies have to be shipped very carefully in special crates. How many crates do the Carsons need to get for these two orders?

   Write all the statements that show how you can figure this out.

2. Mr. Carson is going to get the New York puppies ready. But he can't remember exactly how many that pet store wanted. Mrs. Carson put red ribbons on the

seven puppies that will go to Montana. Mr. Carson knows how many crates he bought. How can he figure out how many puppies to get ready for New York?

Write all the statements that show how he can figure this out. Write both addition and subtraction statements.

3. Mr. Carson has marked the crates for the New York puppies. All the puppies are all out playing in the yard. Mr. Carson wants to bring in the puppies that are going to Montana to groom them, but he can't remember how many are going to Montana. How can he figure out how many puppies with red ribbons he has to find?

Write all the statements that show how he can figure this out. Write both addition and subtraction statements.

Problem D: Mr. Jones and Mrs. Sheltee have decided to combine their classes to do projects on the Civil War.

1. The students have chosen five different projects to do and have decided which books and video tapes each group needs. Mr. Jones has agreed to do the ordering. When the book that the group studying the Rebel Generals has come in, Mr. Jones wants to give Mrs. Sheltee the books her students need. He knows that he has seven books, and that he has four students in his class who are in this group. How can he figure out how many students from Mrs. Sheltee's class are in this group?

Write all the statements that show how he can figure this out. Write both addition and subtraction statements.

2. One day Mr. Jones is absent and the school secretary comes to Mrs. Sheltee to check on how many books they got on the Rebel Generals. That group has been working in Mrs. Sheltee's room so she knows that she has three students in her class in that group and that Mr. Jones has four in that group. She knows that each student has a book. How many books did they get?

Write all the statements that show how she can figure this out.

3. When the project is over, Mrs. Sheltee is going to take the books to the library. She knows she should have seven books. (How does she know that?) She has three books. How many does she still need to collect?

Write all the statements that show how she can figure this out. Write both addition and subtraction statements.

For Multiplication and Division

Parts 1 and 4 of Problem G have the added complexity of requiring some calculations in addition to the ones asked for directly. In Part 1, measurements are given in yards and in feet; the students need to change one to the other. If you have not worked on changing yards to feet or feet to yards, either you should do that before using the problem, or you should change the problem so that all the measurements are given in the same units. (In that case, I recommend using feet because it is the smaller unit and is more common for measurements such as these.)

In Part 4, Nathan gets five bags of 10 balloons. The total number of balloons is needed to do the rest of the problem. Once students understand that they have to find that total themselves, getting to 50 is a quick exercise in skip counting.

Problem E: The Bright Lights Arts Camp has scholarship money for students who want to go but can't afford it. The money comes from the interest earned on a large trust fund given to the camp. The regular scholarships are for $400.00. The treasurer tells the scholarship committee that they have $3,000.00 available for scholarships this year. How many students can get scholarships? Will there be any left over?

Write all the statements that show how they can figure this out. Write both division and multiplication statements.

Problem F: The eleven Hensen County 4-H club junior members who have won the grand prize ribbons for their displays at the county fairs can go to the state fair and stay in the 4-H building for four days. The adult leaders of the Hensen County 4-H club have gotten several owners of food booths at the fair to donate complimentary tickets for the 4-H junior members who will be at the fair. Altogether they got 58 tickets. How many tickets can they give to each junior member? Will there be any tickets left over?

Write all the statements that show how they can figure this out. Write both division and multiplication statements.

Problem G: The soccer team is getting ready for a big playoff game. The stadium they play in has grandstands made of bars with planks for seats.

1. Each section of the grandstand is 30 feet long and 10 sections are connected together on each side of the grandstand. The soccer team wants to put a banner on the bars on the back of the grandstand that is on the street side of the field. Someone has given them 80 yards of banner material that is one yard wide. How many of the sections of the grandstand can the team cover with their banner material if they put it in a straight line?

   Write all the statements that show how they can figure this out. Write both division and multiplication statements.

2. Draw a picture to show how you would use the banner material. Is there any banner material left over?

3. Addition to the problem: Do you think they should use any left-over material to cover a part of one or more sections? Why or why not? If you think they should, add it to your previous picture and describe how much of it you will use and where you put it.

4. Nathan's parents own a store that sells balloons. Nathan has been saving money to get balloons to put on the grandstand on the day of the game. His parents will supply the helium and the strings for the balloons. Nathan is able to get five bags of 10 balloons. Early in the morning of the soccer game, Nathan's dad delivers all of those balloons, filled with helium, to the stadium. The whole team is there to help put them up. After experimenting, the team decides that the balloons look best in groups of three. They need to decide how many groups they will have before deciding where to put them. How can they figure out how many groups of three balloons they will have?

   Write all the statements that show how they can figure this out. Write both division and multiplication statements.

Do the math -

it adds up

Index